12 MINUTES

TO BREAKTHROUGH
Prayer Strategy

MATTIE NOTTAGE

12 MINUTES
TO BREAKTHROUGH
Prayer Strategy

MATTIE NOTTAGE

Copyright © 2016
Mattie Nottage Ministries, Int'l

12 *Minutes to Breakthrough Prayer Strategy*
by Mattie Nottage

Printed in the United States of America
ISBN: 978-0-9896003-5-4

Unless otherwise indicated, all Scripture quotations are taken from the King James Study Bible ©1988 by Liberty University: Thomas Nelson Publishers, Nashville and The Amplified Bible ©1987 by the Zondervan Corporation and the Lockman Foundation, Grand Rapids, Michigan

DEDICATION

This book is dedicated to Holy Spirit who is my Administrator and my life. He is the Incomparable Strategist who has taught me how to gain victory through prayer, fasting and His Word and is the Ultimate Inspiration for this life-changing book. I honor Him because He has blessed me to help arm and equip believers everywhere with powerful spiritual principles. Further, He has anointed me with the ability to train the Body of Christ in the art of strategic prayer and skillful spiritual warfare.

To my best friend, spiritual covering, husband and Senior Pastor, Apostle Edison Nottage: thank you for your continued strength and support. You enable me to be all that I am; for this I am eternally grateful and I will love you from everlasting to everlasting.

And finally to my children and spiritual sons and daughters, you are truly God's greatest miracles.

ACKNOWLEDGEMENTS

First of all, I acknowledge God the Father, Son and Holy Spirit, whose inspiration and anointing led me to write this book as a tool for the deliverance of the nations. I count it an honor to be His servant and chosen vessel.

I would also like to honor God for my grandparents, the late *Reverend Wilfred Johnson and the late Eva Johnson* who, from I was a young girl, were instrumental in teaching me how to pray. They were very influential in helping me to grow spiritually by faithfully driving me to every prayer meeting at our Church while I was growing up. I will always appreciate them both for helping me to become who I am in God today.

To the family of Believers Faith Outreach Ministries in Nassau, Bahamas; Believers Faith Breakthrough Ministries in South Florida; and the friends and partners of Mattie Nottage Ministries International: I am blessed by your prayers and support. Thank you!

INTRODUCTION:
12 MINUTES TO BREAKTHROUGH

YOUR MINUTES TO MIDNIGHT

From time to time everyone will encounter what I call a *midnight season*. During this time you may experience hardships, tragedies and trials which are difficult to overcome. Failure to break free from them can lead to the sabotage of your destiny and may even cause you to lose your direction in life. In this book, I will unveil the secrets of praying during the 12:00 o'clock midnight and noonday hours and how to pray during your midnight seasons.

For some people, when tragedy strikes, prayer is automatic. However, it may not be the first response for others who tend to resort to everything else *except* prayer. I believe that before every midnight or dark event, God gives you some degree of discernment or spiritual intuition where you instinctively know that something is about to happen. God always sends a warning sign before any tragedy hits your life. These perceptions should serve as prophetic indicators alerting you to the urgent need to engage in prayer.

The time when you are facing a calamity is *not* always the ideal time for you to be learning how to pray for a breakthrough. I believe that the moments before your difficult *midnight experiences* should be your time of preparation. These are the times to build yourself spiritually; to learn how to skillfully use your weapons of warfare to bombard heaven; to develop your prayer life to degree where your voice is recognized in heaven and to continually invoke supernatural intervention in your situation.

The Word of God says, ***"No one comes to God except the Holy Spirit draws him."*** In other words, there are times when you will feel the Spirit of God tugging on your heart telling you that you need to pray. Your *minutes to midnight* were the times when the Spirit of God called you into His presence. These were the times there was an unction by Holy Spirit for you to pray; the times He prompted you to read your Bible and other moments He created for you to gain spiritual fortitude and strength.

Your decision to embrace these moments and obey the Spirit of God will determine your spiritual resilience and if you leave every impending battle with victory. Actually, it is during your *minutes to midnight* that the victory is lost or won.

As was His custom, Jesus spent much time in prayer. After every great miracle or times of ministry to the masses, Jesus would withdraw Himself to a quiet place where He would spend time praying to His Heavenly Father. During one of the greatest tests of His life, Jesus knew that the time He spent in prayer in the Garden of Gethsemane before His arrest would be important to His gaining the victory and fulfulling His divine purpose. It was His *moments to midnight;* those times of preparation in prayer that gave Him the power to trust His Father to carry Him through the current challenge He was facing.

¹⁴ *The spirit of a man will sustain his infirmity;...*
(Provbers 18:14)

God seeks to use your *minutes to midnight* to build you spiritually and help gird you for future battles. Your times in prayer during *these times* will determine if you will defeat your giants or if you will see yourself as a grasshopper, when you arrive at the brink of your miracle.

TABLE OF CONTENTS

CHAPTER ONE

LORD, TEACH US TO PRAY

LORD, TEACH US TO PRAY
"...Lord, teach us to pray,..." (Luke 11:1)

One of the greatest blessings to the Body of Christ is the gift of prayer. It is so amazing to me how one of the *most important things in life* that God has designed to rescue people from destructive or tragic situations is now easily being overlooked or, rather, taken for granted.

Most people prefer to spend more time talking, complaining and even crying about their problems than finding time to pray about it. It is said that prayer is the key that can unlock any door and set every captive free. However, so often this vitally important spiritual weapon is given little attention or, even worse, neglected.

Prayer is to the Kingdom of God what money is to the systems of the world. However, prayer should be valued or esteemed greater than money. I say this because many people have placed such a high value on money that they sometimes forget the importance of prayer. The Word of God states that money answers all things; however, you should not esteem money above prayer.

Prayer is the force that keeps the things of the kingdom activated in the life of the believer. The power of prayer allows persons in one region to effect change in another. Prayer has the power to accomplish in the earthly realm what no other force, including money, is able to achieve. Prayer has power; moreover, effective, fervent prayer has power.

The Greek word for Prayer is **proseuche,** which can be defined as **communion or communication with God.** Communication is interaction that involves the exchange of information between you and God. Primarily, this conversation is initiated because dialogue or resolve is desired. The conversation can begin wherein both parties exchange information and give input based on how the conversation is going. *Similarly, so it is with prayer.*

As you continue to engage in consistent, frequent communication with God, you will begin to grow in the things of God, learn His voice and discern His will for your life. Therefore a well-developed prayer life is essential to your overall spiritual development and maturity.

CONSISTENCY IN PRAYER

Consistency in prayer is having an unwavering specified mode of communicating with God which is continually developed. It is a clearly defined routine that is repeated constantly and regularly in order to accomplish one's spiritual goals.

Your consistent development in prayer initiates conversations with God, activates heaven to move on your behalf and cultivates a powerful connection that gives you, the believer, a divine support system while here on earth.

These are some of the things that consistent fervent prayer has the power to do:
- *Consistent Prayer of Breakthrough* has the power to bring divine healing even when your doctor cannot help you.

- *Consistent Prayer of Breakthrough* has the power to destroy addictions even when rehabilitation falls short.

- *Consistent Prayer of Breakthrough* repairs broken relationships, families and marriages even when they appear hopeless.

- *Consistent Prayer of Breakthrough* delivers the wounded soul and brings peace of mind.

- *Consistent Prayer of Breakthrough* has the power to break the yoke of financial bondage and hardship, positioning you to walk in wealth and prosperity.

- *Consistent Prayer of Breakthrough* has the power to change ungodly laws and enact new righteous laws.

- *Consistent Prayer of Breakthrough* has the power to cause dreams, visions and ideas to manifest despite all odds.

- *Consistent Prayer of Breakthrough* will attract the ***fire of God*** to you and ignite the fire of God within you.

- *Consistent Prayer of Breakthrough* will push you towards the ***fire of God*** in order to activate your purpose in God. ***(Exodus 3:4)***

- *Consistent Prayer of Breakthrough* will cause the ***fire of God*** to burn through you. You become a fiery blaze for God changing people's lives everywhere.

(See more on The Benefits of Prayer in Chapter Ten)

In short, when you are able to pray consistently and effectively, you become empowered to activate kingdom laws and principles. This includes laws of healing, life, prosperity, wealth and other benefits that are already in existence in the spiritual realm. That is why when you pray, you should always ask that the will of God be done ***"...in earth, as it has already been done in heaven." (Matthew 6:10)***

THE PRAYER ESSENTIAL

Prayer is essential to every believer's life just as water is essential to the life of a fish and breath is to every human being. It is therefore incumbent upon every believer to spend quality time in prayer every day, even if it is only for ***12 minutes*** at a time.

Prayer is the only spiritual weapon that can be both offensive and defensive. Prayer can lock or bind the demonic realm; it can also unlock the supernatural realm of God, giving you victory in every area of your life.

As you embark on your spiritual journey with God you will recognize that consistent prayer is vitally important to your overall growth and development.

In **Luke 18:1–5** the Word of God encourages us to pray without ceasing:

> *¹ And he (Jesus) spake a parable unto them to this end, that men ought always to pray, and not to faint;*
>
> *² Saying, There was in a city a judge, which feared not God, neither regarded man:*
>
> *³ And there was a widow in that city; and she came unto him, saying, Avenge me of mine adversary.*
>
> *⁴ And he would not for a while: but afterward he said within himself, Though I fear not God, nor regard man;*
>
> *⁵ Yet because this widow troubleth me, I will avenge her, lest by her continual coming she weary me.*

Jesus spoke this parable specifically about a woman facing a difficult legal battle before an unjust judge. She did not know how she would gain the victory yet, due to her continual petitioning before the judge, he eventually ruled in her favor.

Likewise, Jesus wants you to have the same kind of persistence and consistent faith concerning God's kingdom, your life and family. He wants your faith in Him to be consistent, steadfast and strong.

> *⁶ But without faith it is impossible to please him: for he that cometh to God must believe that he is, and that he is a rewarder of them that diligently seek him.*
> *(Hebrews 11:6)*

If you are going to have power over your circumstances, you must learn how to engage the weapon of prayer. Further, you must believe that God exists, that He is the answer to your dilemma, and that He rewards those who diligently seek Him.

Faith is having confidence in God. No matter what you are going through in life, if you see God as your only source and relentlessly pursue Him, you will then begin to have unprecedented breakthroughs.

PRAYING IN TONGUES

Likewise the Spirit also helpeth our infirmities: for we know not what we should pray for as we ought: but the Spirit itself maketh intercession for us with groanings which cannot be uttered.
(Romans 8:26)

The Word of God reveals that the Spirit makes intercession for us with groanings which cannot be uttered. Praying in Tongues is the same as praying in the Spirit. This type of prayer is accessible to everyone who has been baptized in the Holy Spirit. *(See Prayer to Receive the Baptism of The Holy Ghost pg. 184)*

Speaking in tongues is one of the evidences that you are filled with the Holy Ghost and that He is at work on the inside of you. When you pray in Tongues you pray mysteries and the will of God through utterances inspired only by the Holy Spirit.

15 "What is it then? I will pray with the spirit, and I will pray with the understanding also..."
(1 Corinthians 14:15a)

Since your mind or your own understanding is not directly involved in this type of prayer, it can be said that the outcome you achieve as a result of praying in Tongues in the realm of the Spirit far exceeds that of your intellect or that which you can comprehend.

Further, when you pray in the Spirit, you are praying in a heavenly language, unknown to your human mind but understood by the Spirit of God. It is at this time that you are praying in the Spirit, groaning in a language unknown to self but understood by God that is also called *a heavenly language.*

At this point deep is calling unto deep; you can feel the Spirit of God drawing you closer and closer to the presence of God where you become totally broken and yielded. It is the outpouring of the soul an intimate exchange between you and God.

You cannot measure the power of your tongue by what is said in the English language or your native tongue. There is so much more to experience once you have been filled with the blessed Holy Ghost with the evidence of speaking in tongues.

There are depths and realms in the spirit which can only be attained by praying the language of Holy Spirit. Your ability to experience these realms and dimensions cannot be taught nor are they automatically inherited. They can only be accessed through the power of Holy Spirit.

With the plan of salvation, you must ask Holy Spirit to come and dwell on the inside of you. Your next step is to ask Him to baptize you with His fire and give you proof that He is there by causing you to speak in heavenly tongues, which is His language. Everything in God's kingdom happens by faith, so is being baptized in the Holy Ghost.

Cultivating the Fruit While Activating The Gifts of The Spirit

²² But the fruit of the Spirit is love, joy, peace, longsuffering, gentleness, goodness, faith,

²³ Meekness, temperance:...
(Galatians 5:22–23)

Whenever you practice praying in your heavenly language, you will see the fruit of the spirit maturing in your life. In **Galatians 5**, Paul identifies the attributes present in the life of someone manifesting the *Fruit of the Spirit*. In 1 Corinthians 12:7-11, he teaches us about the gifts of the Spirit and how they are all given to us by one same Spirit.

⁴ Now there are diversities of gifts, but the same Spirit.

⁵ And there are differences of administrations, but the same Lord.

⁶ And there are diversities of operations, but it is the same God which worketh all in all.

⁷ But the manifestation of the Spirit is given to every man to profit withal.

⁸ For to one is given by the Spirit the word of wisdom; to another the word of knowledge by the same Spirit;

⁹ To another faith by the same Spirit; to another the gifts of healing by the same Spirit;

¹⁰ To another the working of miracles; to another prophecy; to another discerning of spirits; to another divers kinds of tongues; to another the interpretation of tongues:

¹¹ But all these worketh that one and the selfsame Spirit, dividing to every man severally as he will.
(1 Corinthians 12:4–11)

The gifts of the Spirit are given to us to uplift and build the Body of Christ *(Ephesians 4:11-12)*. However in order to further grow and develop the fruit and gifts of the Spirit you must be willing to speak the language of the Holy Spirit. Praying in Tongues connects you with the realm of the Spirit and it is from this realm that the gifts of the spirit become activated; they flow out of you like a fountain of living waters.

The Secret of Speaking in Tongues To Receive A Word of Knowledge

Many times people ask me how do I know details about people when I am praying for them. I tell them that I do not know details until Holy Spirit reveals them to me. As I mentioned earlier, one of the ways this can happen is by speaking the language of Holy Spirit.

When you speak His language He reveals to you His thoughts and secrets. Then you simply translate it back into the language of the person who needs help and deliverance. As the Word of Knowledge concerning the person is spoken then they are able to get a clear understanding that God knows what they are going through and they then become eager to receive their miracle from Him.

A SIGN FROM GOD

God uses many signs to show or demonstrate His power. A sign is a prophetic pointer that the Spirit of God is present to save, heal and deliver. The sign is given to point or draw you back to God. Speaking in tongues is also a sign from God that the Holy Spirit is present.

"...they shall speak with new tongues;"
(Mark 16:17)

He that believeth on me, as the scripture
hath said, out of his belly shall flow
rivers of living water.
(John 7:38)

On the day of Pentecost as over 120 believers gathered to worship and pray, the Holy Ghost descended on each of them with cloven tongues which seemed like fire. No doubt the believers were looking forward to the moment when the Holy Spirit would enter but no one anticipated the move of God they experienced.

[1]And when the day of Pentecost was fully come,
they were all with one accord in one place.

> *² And suddenly there came a sound from heaven as of a rushing mighty wind, and it filled all the house where they were sitting.*
>
> *³ And there appeared unto them cloven tongues like as of fire, and it sat upon each of them.*
> *(Acts 2:1-3)*

The Word of God reveals that they all began to speak in other tongues once the Holy Ghost came upon them and gave them utterance.

> *⁴ And they were all filled with the Holy Ghost, and began to speak with other tongues, as the Spirit gave them utterance.*
> *(Acts 2:4)*

The Word of God further reveals that although there were people there from various nations, everyone present heard the believers speaking in their own native language. This phenomenal move of the Holy Spirit sparked a mighty revival that led to thousands being converted in one day.

There are various benefits of speaking in Tongues or praying in the Spirit which include the following:

1. It gives us direct communication with God as we speak to Him. *(1 Corinthians 14:4)*

2. It builds you up by strengthening your inner man.

3. It is a sign of the new birth and the infilling of the Holy Spirit in the life of a believer.

4. Praying in the Spirit teaches you *the way of the Spirit of God* as it opens your spirit more to the presence and power of God.

5. It ultimately empowers you to discern the will of God and recognize His voice.

6. It allows you to pray mysteries unto God through the Spirit of God which causes supernatural mysteries to become unveiled and hidden revelations to immediately unfold. *(Ephesians 3:4-5; Matthew 13:13-17)*

7. It enables you to instruct God's angels to fight on your behalf or instruct fallen angels to back up and flee in the name of Jesus. *(1 Corinthians 13:1; Psalm 103:20)*

8. It releases the will of God to manifest in your life.

9. It opens your spirit to further receive the truth and can give you spiritual power to live victoriously. *(1 Corinthians 12:7-13)*

10. It helps your weakness, giving you spiritual strength as it unctions the Holy Spirit to make intercession for you. *(Romans 8:26, 27)*

11. It brings comfort to your soul, which is comprised of your mind, will, intellect and emotions.

12. It teaches you and causes you to recall everything that you have learned. *(John 14:26)*

PRAYING THE WORD

One of the most powerful weapons that adds dimension to your prayer is when you pray the Word of God. Christians can use the Word of God as a weapon on a daily basis. The Word is a lamp and light for guidance but it also is a sword that can kill and heal.

> *⁸ This book of the law shall not depart out of thy mouth; but thou shalt meditate therein day and night, that thou mayest observe to do according to all that is written therein: for then thou shalt make thy way prosperous, and then thou shalt have good success. (Joshua 1:8)*

We are commanded to meditate on the Word day and night *(Psalm 1:2)*. Further, when you pray the Word of God you are praying for the will of the Father to be done in earth, even as it is being done in heaven. Therefore, the Word of God should direct our praying.

God will respond to His Word. The scriptures reveal the extent to which God is committed to honoring His Word, namely that: the Word will not return to Him void *(Isaiah 55:11)*; God hastens His Word to perform it *(Jeremiah 1:12)* and God has magnified His Word above all His name *(Psalm 138:2)*.

> *¹Then was Jesus led up of the Spirit into the wilderness to be tempted of the devil.*
>
> *² And when he had fasted forty days and forty nights, he was afterward an hungered.*

3 And when the tempter came to him, he said, If thou be the Son of God, command that these stones be made bread.

4 But he answered and said, It is written, Man shall not live by bread alone, but by every word that proceedeth out of the mouth of God.

5 Then the devil taketh him up into the holy city, and setteth him on a pinnacle of the temple,

6 And saith unto him, If thou be the Son of God, cast thyself down: for it is written, He shall give his angels charge concerning thee: and in their hands they shall bear thee up, lest at any time thou dash thy foot against a stone.

7 Jesus said unto him, It is written again, Thou shalt not tempt the Lord thy God.

In **Matthew 4:1–7** Jesus demonstrated that declaring the Word of God is a direct counterattack against the enemy. As He was tested by the devil His first response to every temptation was, *"It is written..."*

In order to be armed and fully equipped to declare the Word we must know and study the Word of God. We must hide it in our hearts **(Psalm 119:11)**.

IT'S ALL IN THE SEEK!

Oftentimes people ask me "Why **12 Minutes To Breakthrough**? Why not **12 years** to breakthrough? Why not **50 years** to breakthrough?" I simply tell them that God is accelerating His work in the lives of His people and He is doing it swiftly in the realm of the spirit.

²¹ Yea, whiles I was speaking in prayer, even the man Gabriel, whom I had seen in the vision at the beginning, being caused to fly swiftly, touched me about the time of the evening oblation. (Daniel 9:21)

I discovered **12 Minutes To Breakthrough** when our church began to experience the Glory of God in powerful ways. When the Lord spoke to us about the glory we soon saw manifestations of His presence in our midst. We saw the glory of God demonstrated during our time of worship, intercession and seek as we waited on Him. We soon realized that God was doing something totally different amongst us.

My Personal Seek

Months prior the Spirit of the Lord had called me into a time of consecration before Him. Initially I was compelled to commence a 3-night sabbatical. During this **72-hour period** the Spirit of the Lord impressed upon me that He wanted to do a greater work through me. This prompting by Holy Spirit led me to over seven months on the altar before Him and now, almost a year later, I am still finding myself retreating to this secret place with Him.

Although this time on the altar was priceless and precious to me, it required almost total isolation from everything and everyone that I loved or was familiar with. I sacrificed time with my family and home. I gave up everything because I wanted more of God. Sometimes when you desire something great to happen in your life it requires a greater seek.

> ### Sacrifice On The Altar Of God Always Ushers In The Glory!

Then The Glory Comes

Glory is the essence, character, person and presence of Almighty God. The glory of God came without measure and began falling in our church in ways unimaginable as the Spirit of God drew scores of people into our services.

Miracles, signs and wonders occurred in almost every service. Deaf ears opened; shortened limbs instantaneously grew out; several women were delivered from the spirit of barrenness and eventually gave birth to beautiful babies.

Deliverance began happening as more and more people began to cry out to be set free from evil spirits. Moreover, people were delivered from demonic attacks and healed from all manner of sickness and disease, such as: cancer, lumps, tumors and more.

Many people experienced supernatural weight loss instantaneously during the service while others received supernatural debt cancellation and found monies added to their bank accounts. All of this occurred because the grace of God was extended to us. My husband and I, along with our entire membership, prayed and fasted for almost 15 years for God to reveal and release His glory amongst us.

We also saw peculiar signs and wonders such as the supernatural oil and gold dust from heaven appearing on the worshippers, while precious stones, pearls, crystals and diamonds also manifested during our services. Along with these supernatural occurrences, angels were visibly seen as the glory cloud descended. However, one of the greatest miracles was the souls that were saved and people who received the baptism of the Holy Spirit with fire.

GREAT WARFARE MEANS GREAT GLORY

Whenever God is doing something great the enemy always shows up. Although the glory of God had manifested in many powerful ways during our Revival services, I noticed that many people were not maintaining their breakthroughs.

To some degree, these persons could not receive their breakthrough on a natural level or by their own strength but needed supernatural intervention by the Spirit of God. However, He also revealed to me that there were some things that the people themselves would have to do in order to realize and maintain their deliverance. They would leave the service victorious to resume their daily lives; however, many would soon forget what God supernaturally did for them.

Eventually they were again attacked by the enemy but were not prepared for the assault and found themselves in the same oppressive situation from which they had previously been delivered.

"...sin no more, lest a worse thing come unto thee." (John 5:14b)

Jesus tells a man whom He had delivered from a thirty-eight year long infirmity to go his way and sin no more so that something worse would not come upon his life. Many people end up in the same or worse demonic condition from which they had been delivered because they did not do the practical things needed in order to maintain their deliverance neither did they obey the spiritual instructions given.

For example, I would encourage some people to separate themselves from environments which I discerned were harmful to their overall process of deliverance. Some people disregarded the instructions and chose to stay where they were. Eventually, they became overtaken by the demonic forces in that area. Unfortunately, their fall was even worse than their previous dilemma.

Holy Spirit then revealed to me that these vicious cycles were perpetuated by *stubborn problems* held in place by demonic strongmen that were unwilling to leave.

43 When the unclean spirit is gone out of a man, he walketh through dry places, seeking rest, and findeth none.

44 Then he saith, I will return into my house from whence I came out; and when he is come, he findeth it empty, swept, and garnished.

45 Then goeth he, and taketh with himself seven other spirits more wicked than himself, and they enter in and dwell there: and the last state of that man is worse than the first. Even so shall it be also unto this wicked generation. (Matthew 12:43–45)

In ***Matthew 12:43–45***, the Word of God reveals that whenever someone is delivered from an unclean spirit, the spirit is cast out but comes back, at another time to see if it can regain habitation in that person's life. If that person has not spent time building up themselves spiritually then they remain vulnerable to the attacks of the enemy.

Therefore, it is every person's responsibility to continue to engage the battle on their own behalf in order to maintain their victory. Personal time should be spent reading the Word and praying, so that every void can be filled with the presence of God.

After gaining this revelation, it was then that Holy Spirit unveiled a solution to this spiritual dilemma called, ***The 12 Minutes To Breakthrough Prayer Strategy.***

His strategy was simple: when you pray in the Spirit for **12** days at **12** noon and **12** midnight you are guaranteed to build spiritual momentum, see results and receive total breakthrough. I asked Him why and He said, ***"I always send my angel of breakthrough and deliverance whenever you pray this type of radical prayer."***

CLARION CALL TO THE MIDNIGHT PRAYER

When the Spirit of the Lord revealed this powerful prayer strategy for breakthrough to me, I immediately sounded a clarion call to my team of Intercessors. I shared with them what the Spirit of God had spoken to me concerning the **Midnight Prayer.**

With this assignment Holy Spirit also gave me strict instructions to which everyone would have to adhere. He told me to lead the Intercessors through a very intense, radical warfare prayer and praise regimen for **12 minutes**. He stipulated that everyone was required to sign in and the doors were to be locked promptly at 11:55 p.m.

At first I felt that only **12** persons would respond or even show up at the sanctuary. However, to my surprise desperate people came from everywhere bringing their entire families. What further surprised me was that many who did not make the 11:55 p.m. deadline faithfully remained outside of the sanctuary doors warfaring in prayer and participating in whatever training practices they heard through the doors.

For **12 days** I led them through a rigorous spiritual warfare training and prayer boot camp. The miracles that happened after the prayer were totally amazing, to say the least; people began receiving immediate, supernatural breakthroughs and testimonies began pouring in from everywhere. I then understood that people were desperate and were prepared to do whatever it took to receive a breakthrough in their lives.

CHAPTER TWO

I NEED A BREAKTHROUGH

SPECIAL NOTE
"Before you can ever experience a total breakthrough; sometimes you may need to break down, break out, break open, break beyond, break forth, break in...then eventually, breakthrough!"

WHAT IS A BREAKTHROUGH?

"And David came to Baalperazim, and David smote them there, and said, The LORD hath broken forth upon mine enemies before me, as the breach of waters. Therefore he called the name of that place Baalperazim." (2 Samuel 5:20)

The Greek word for breakthrough is **epanastasi,** which means to break out or to break beyond; to break free from; to overflow; to overturn all that is in your way and coming out victorious.

In **2 Samuel 5** David faced one of the greatest challenges of his military career. As soon as his enemies, the Philistines, heard that David had been anointed as king, they devised an attack against him. In desperation, David went before the Lord to receive instruction as to how to overthrow his enemies.

During his time of devotion the Spirit of God assured him that he was to pursue his enemy and he would, no doubt, come out victorious. Empowered with a military strategy from God and assured of victory, David gathered his men and pursued the Philistines. As the Lord had promised, David was victorious in the battle and defeated his enemy.

In gratitude to God and as a memorial David named the place **Baal-perazim**, which is translated **Lord of the Breakthrough**, because he ascribed the ultimate victory to God. In short, David was acknowledging that God was the One who gave him the military power to overwhelm his enemies and gain the victory that day.

WHY IS A BREAKTHROUGH NECESSARY?

"What are you tired of? Are you more physically tired that you cannot pray for 12 minutes or are you tired of your situation?"

For years we have heard of phenomenal breakthroughs occurring in various arenas such as science and technology, medicine, economics and others. Historically, these documented breakthroughs or modern day inventions have served to improve the lives of people. The invention of electricity, the light bulb, penicillin, the telephone, the Internet and others have all helped to improve man's overall health and well-being.

Now, however, God is calling His people to experience breakthroughs in the realm of the spirit which will demonstrate a greater level of God's glory and power here on earth.

The Lord began to speak to me one day when I was conducting the midday prayer services which had evolved from being dedicated to prayer only into a full service which included: miracles, healing and deliverance. I was very grateful that God was moving powerfully during the services but He said to me, "If my people are going to have sustained victory, if they are going to break through to the next level of victory, they are going to have to learn how to pray."

Then He showed me that some people's miracles are short-lived because they have not fully broken through to the next level that God had prepared for them. Some people got or received a miracle but never did what was necessary to sustain their miracle. He said because if they do not completely breakthrough, they sometimes firnd themselves locked in old cycles which they should have already surpassed. Each person has been created by God to accomplish certain things within a specified season. If you remain stuck in a past season this can lead to years of frustration, fear and anxiety.

It is vitally important that you seek God through prayer to begin to breakthrough in every area of your life. He said in **John 10:10** that He came to give us life and life more abundantly and He wants to be your God of the Breakthrough.

GOD OF THE BREAKTHROUGH

God is a God of Breakthrough. During times of hardship and difficulty when it seems as though God is not there, this generally occurs because God will go before you in the way and make provisions for your victory.

One of the attributes of God is that He is Jehovah Jireh, typically known as the One who provides. However, as Jireh this means that God will see to it that every need you have is met or that everything you need is provided. *(Genesis 22:14)*

He goes before you as a mighty Man of War to break down walls, dismantle gates and remove demonic hindrances or obstructions out of your pathway. He will fight on your behalf or do whatever it takes to make provision for you.

> *13 And it came to pass, when Joshua was by Jericho, that he lifted up his eyes and looked, and, behold, there stood a man over against*

him with his sword drawn in his hand: and Joshua went unto him, and said unto him, Art thou for us, or for our adversaries?

14 And he said, Nay; but as captain of the host of the LORD am I now come. And Joshua fell on his face to the earth, and did worship, and said unto him, What saith my Lord unto his servant?

15 And the captain of the LORD's host said unto Joshua, Loose thy shoe from off thy foot; for the place whereon thou standest is holy. And Joshua did so. (Joshua 5:13–15)

Joshua, was a man of war who was facing a major battle against his enemy in Jericho. Jericho was known to be an impregnable city due to the width of its massive walls. However, God had told Joshua that He had given Him the city of Jericho and that they were to go and possess it.

Prior to the battle against Jericho, Joshua had a divine encounter with what appeared to be a man with his sword drawn. Joshua unknowingly confronted a mighty warrior angel who, I believe, was one of the captains over the battalion of breakthrough angels.

Intolerant of any potential enemy, Joshua demanded to know which side he was on. The angel identified himself as the captain of the host of the Lord's army. This angel sent from the throne room of God as a sign to Joshua that God would give him the victory in this battle.

As Joshua and his army followed God's instructions by praising and marching around Jericho, the breakthrough angles toppled the walls of that impregnable city. That day, Joshua and the children of Israel glorified God once again for giving them this breakthrough and victory.

"The right hand of the LORD is exalted:
the right hand of the LORD doeth valiantly."
(Psalm 118:16)

ANGELS CALLED BREAKTHROUGH

God dispatches His hosts of angels to perform various functions on behalf of mankind. There are messenger angels, miracle angels, warrior angels, breakthrough angels and a whole host of other angels which stand ready to accomplish the will of God in the earth.

I believe that God's breakthrough angels are also warrior angels who fight to bring the promises of God to pass in your life. These robust angels are protectors who show up during times of war to set ambushments in the enemy's camp or break through demonic resistance against the people of God. I believe that these breakthrough angels took the wheels off of the chariots of Pharaoh's army who pursued the Children of Israel after they left Egypt.

I also believe that it was these angels along with others which confused the armies of the enemy who had set themselves in a great battle against King Jehoshaphat.

How To Recognize Breakthrough Angels

Breakthrough angels like all other angels hearken to the voice of God's commands. Whenever you pray, worship and call upon God, especially during difficult situations, these breakthrough angels show up. They possess war-like characteristics and may appear to be spiritually aggressive. Every time I have had an encounter with them, they appear to be robust and very strong.

I can remember conducting a Revival service, several years ago, in the Turks and Caicos Islands. I can recall that it was extremely difficult to deliver the Word on the first night as I discerned a strong demonic resistance. It was only the first night and I felt like closing the meeting.

That night, I went back to my hotel and prayed until I eventually fell into a deep sleep. At about 3:00 am I had a vision and in the vision the Spirit of God showed me a huge principality spirit that sat over the island and the Church where I was ministering. It had the face of a man but looked like a big monster made out of rock. I recognized it as a **rock of religion**, or a strong religious spirit that manipulates and controls people's minds making them rebellious to the truth. They resist or oppose change and feel comfortable in their carnal state.

In the vision, I tried everything to move this spirit, but just stayed there fastened in its position. I decided to intensify in prayer and eventually I saw the rock beginning to crumble. I then realized that my prayer had activated the supernatural realm and God dispatched an angel of breakthrough that pushed the rock all the way back into the ocean and destroyed it.

The next two nights of the Revival were powerful and God moved mightily as supernatural miracles of healing and deliverance began happening throughout the entire building.

Whenever these **angels of breakthrough** show up they usually do so with much fanfare and generally shift the atmosphere. These power fighter angels are dispatched to deliver the people of God during challenging times or various hardships. Further, as you begin to pray and praise, God dispatches this battalion of angels to warfare on your behalf.

Break In or Breakthrough?

God said that many people were breaking into a new dimension but they were not breaking through. The difference between a **break-in** and a **breakthrough** is that with a break in the only thing that happens is you enter into something but nothing else may be accomplished. However, when you experience a breakthrough, you are able to go beyond every limitation, defeat your enemy and emerge victorious.

Once you have broken beyond your barriers, you come out of your deliverance with new revelations, new testimonies or a new sense of purpose and as a result, you experience some level of change. *This is what I call a paradigm shift.*

> **Never Go Through Something For Nothing;**
> **Always Come Out With Something...**

One evening, shortly before midnight I was faced with a very difficult dilemma and began crying out to God for immediate intervention.   In the midst of my travail I heard Holy Spirit to me, *"Just take **12 minutes** and you will have your breakthrough"*. He said to me that if I was really desperate for the miracle I was pleading with Him to perform; I would arise and get into His presence for **12** minutes.

He asked, *"Are you more physically tired that you cannot pray for 12 minutes or are you tired of your situation?"* Then I heard Him say, *"I guarantee you that after those 12 minutes you are going to have a breakthrough"*.

BREAKING THROUGH THE ENEMY'S LINES

The only way a true breakthrough can happen is if you engage the spirit realm of God through fervent and sustained prayer. A breakthrough immediately advances you into the enemy's territory and allows you to penetrate the enemy's front-line of defense. It is forceful and generally occurs without warning.

When you break through you overthrow and defeat your enemy, suddenly. God has predetermined an unexpected breakthrough for you when you grab His attention during the ***12 Minutes To Breakthrough Prayer Routine.***

This is a right now, intense, radical, spontaneous, active prayer of action that demands immediate results. It is a prayer for the desperate, those who need a **right now** breakthrough from God. This **12 Minutes To Breakthrough Prayer Strategy** is for sharpshooters praying specific warfare prayers against demonic strongholds.

In **2 Samuel 23:15–16** the Word of God records how David, who was in the midst of a fierce battle with the Philistines, desired some water to drink. Knowing the severe battle in which they were engaged, the Philistines encamped around the only water source available to both armies for miles.

As a diabolical battle strategy, and knowing that David and his men would eventually need water to drink, the Philistines planned a surprise attack on David and his men should they attempt to draw water from the well.

> **15 And David longed, and said, Oh that one would give me drink of the water of the well of Bethlehem, which is by the gate!**
>
> **16 And the three mighty men brake through the host of the Philistines, and drew water out of the well of Bethlehem, that was by the gate, and took it, and brought it to David: nevertheless he would not drink thereof, but poured it out unto the Lord.**
> **(2 Samuel 23:15–16)**

A lot of times people want a breakthrough or a miracle from God but they want God to do everything for them. While there is nothing impossible for God to do, He desires that you are involved in what He is doing in your life. In other words, you must believe Him then act upon His Word, in faith.

The word **koinonia,** in Greek means *communion, relationship or joint participation.* When you engage in the **12 Minutes to Breakthrough Strategy** you work along with Holy Spirit to bring about your breakthrough and the enemy's defeat. God is saying I am now bringing you to the place of spiritual enlightenment but I want you to understand the reason why I am waking you at this hour.

THE PRAYER WARRIOR'S BREAKTHROUGH

"Set A Watch And Wait!"

Even though David was a skilled warrior and king he always sought specific instructions from God as to how to deal with his enemies before going into any battle. In **2 Samuel 5:17-19** the Bible records a confrontation between King David and his arch enemies, the Philistines:

> *¹⁷ But when the Philistines heard that they had anointed David king over Israel, all the Philistines came up to seek David; and David heard of it, and went down to the hold.*

> *¹⁸ The Philistines also came and spread themselves in the valley of Rephaim.*

> *¹⁹ And David enquired of the Lord, saying, Shall I go up to the Philistines? wilt thou deliver them into mine hand? And the Lord said unto David, Go up: for I will doubtless deliver the Philistines into thine hand. (2 Samuel 5:17–19)*

It is important to note that it was not until the Philistines heard that God had anointed David to be king that they intensified their warfare against him. **You are** *never a threat to the enemy until he recognizes your anointing.*

David obtained total victory in that battle and called the place **Baal-perazim** because he experienced a level of breakthrough over his enemies. Not only did God instruct David to destroy his enemies, He also gave him instructions to burn and destroy their images.

> **Always Destroy Your Enemy's Idols, Lest Your Children Rise Up To Worship Them!**

Although David had previously defeated an army of Philistines, another sector of the Philistine army rose up against him and this time they were fiercer than the army before them. David had to seek God once again as to what he should do, as he was not prepared to use the same strategy that he had used to defeat the first army.

> **22 The Philistines came up again and spread themselves out in the Valley of Rephaim.**
>
> **23 When David inquired of the Lord, He said, You shall not go up, but go around behind them and come upon them over opposite the mulberry (or balsam) trees.**
>
> **24 And when you hear the sound of marching in the tops of the mulberry trees, then bestir yourselves, for then has the Lord gone out before you to smite the army of the Philistines.**
>
> **25 And David did as the Lord had commanded him, and smote the Philistines from Geba to Gezer. (2 Samuel 5:22-25 AMP)**

This time God told David to reposition his army behind the enemy but not to move until he heard the sound of marching on the tops of the mulberry trees. God was giving David specific instructions for a battle watch. Setting the compass meant that they would have to implement a shrewd battle strategy in the face of this aggravating enemy.

As people normally use a compass to give guidance and directives for their journey, even so, in the spiritual realm, God wants you to set a spiritual compass of prayer that will guide you to your ultimate breakthrough. During your seasons of intense battles God will give you a battle strategy or a prayer watch to defeat your enemy. David completely obeyed the spiritual warfare tactic from God and completely defeated his enemy.

You must seek God for divine instructions if you are going to gain any level of victory in your life as you face various hardships. Many times you are faced with dilemmas that may require help from another dimension. In these situations, as you cry out to God in prayer, the Spirit of God may employ **angels of breakthrough** to fight on your behalf.

CHAPTER THREE

IT'S TIME TO PRAY!

PREPARATION AND PERSISTENCE PAYS

Whenever you are faced with any challenge or tragedy, as a believer you cannot just lie down and die. You must engage yourself in spiritual battle so that you can win the war. This may require you developing a counterattack against your enemy and intensifying the use of your spiritual weapons of declaring the Word, praise, worship and, most of all, prayer; even if it means waking up crying out to God at midnight!

This consistent preparation through prayer is vitally important because many people in the Body of Christ are dry, stagnant and void of spiritual power and enlightenment. Unfortunately, many in the Body of Christ do not understand the power that is available to them through developing a prayer life. Prayer is the key that gives every believer direct access to the throne room of God.

The purpose of praying any prayer is to receive God's answers, not man's opinions, about what you are going through. Your persistent prayer pays, as it causes God to send the answer. Your decision to pray is a clear indication to God that you realize you are faced with a dilemma or situation that requires answers from a higher realm.

Prayer must be the epicenter of your daily routine if you are going to live a victorious life. As a custom, even Jesus prayed every day while on earth. Further, he lived a lifestyle of communing with His Father concerning everything. You must begin to see prayer as an essential part of our kingdom culture, as believers, and as a powerful weapon given to us by God.

When faced with various dilemmas, many believers tend to find themselves trapped in demonic cycles of perplexity, frustration and confusion. As a citizen of the Kingdom of God, you cannot turn to the systems of the world or even the kingdom of darkness for answers to your problems. You must see God as your only source. The only way that you will receive true answers and obtain absolute resolve is by engaging the spiritual weapon of prayer.

SPIRITUAL FRUSTRATION
What is spiritual frustration?

Spiritual frustration is a state or condition of discomfort or dissatisfaction where you may find that you are not in the spiritual position you should be in God. Spiritual frustration occurs whenever you become overwhelmed and overtaken by the affairs of life. These *affairs* can move you further and further away from the things of God causing you to become spiritually weak. In this state of spiritual vulnerability you may become easily distracted, irritated or annoyed by everything, even the smallest matters.

The difference between natural frustration and spiritual frustration is that the root of natural frustration is seated in *physical* or *natural* problems.

On the other hand, the root of spiritual frustration is anchored in your lack of spiritual engagement in prayer and the things of God. Most people blame their spiritual frustration on external factors, however, if the truth were told, it really exists because there is a spiritual void in their life.

Every believer at some point in their walk with God may find themselves *spiritually frustrated.* Others who *do not* experience spiritual frustration are generally comfortable, passive Christians who have maladapted to mediocrity and are satisfied *with* the way their life is going. These are who I call "shore-line" or carnal Christians who are satisfied with just being saved. They do not desire to grow spiritually or experience more in God.

Spiritual frustration generally occurs in people who believe that the Hand of God is on their lives but they find themselves out of spiritual alignment. These people desire to be used of God and are fully aware that they must do whatever is necessary to realign themselves with the perfect will of God. If you ever find yourself spiritually frustrated you must begin to devise an aggressive prayer strategy to restore your relationship with God.

Are You Doing A Good Thing Or A God Thing

Spiritually frustrated people often become distracted and consumed by the cares of this life and do not spend adequate time grooming and enhancing their spiritual man. Therefore, the enemy cleverly overwhelms them keeping them spiritually void and depraved; causing much stress and fatigue.

> ### *The Stronger Your Spiritual Man,*
> ### *The More You Will Desire The Things Of God.*

For the believer who truly loves God, He can choose to be overtaken by the enemy or become spiritually frustrated with where they are and do something about it.

I know this may seem like an oxymoron but on the other hand, I also believe that spiritual frustration is an indication that the Holy Spirit is dealing with you and desires you to come closer into the Presence of God. He allows you to become spiritually frustrated to let you know that your spirit man is weak and needs to be strengthened and refueled in His presence. He wants you to trust him totally and not lean to your own understanding.

Unfortunately, if you do not do what is necessary to break away into the presence of God, this perpetual spiritual depravity can eventually lead to backsliding and spiritual death. Your ultimate spiritual demise forfeits you from becoming who God had originally called you to be and losing the blessings that He had for you.

God has called you to be blessed and not overwhelmed by cares. You are destined for greatness; you must exercise your spiritual tools of prayer, studying the Word, worship and others to continually cultivate the presence of God in your life.

SIGNS OF SPIRITUAL FRUSTRATION

Spiritual frustration will cause you to lose your place in God. When you are spiritually frustrated, this

---

greatly challenges your faith and the anointing of God on your life.

As a believer you must not allow yourself to become overwhelmed by the cares of life to the point where you become spiritually frustrated. ***There are a number of factors which determine whether or not you are experiencing a degree of spiritual frustration, some of which include:***

- **Irritability** – you find yourself at the place where you are very easily irritated by virtually everything to the point that you begin to snap at the smallest matter.

- **Unhappiness** – you find yourself sad while everyone around you is happy or laughing and you are unable to conceal your sadness or displeasure.

- **Restlessness** – you tend to feel unsettled and no matter how hard you try, a nagging sense that you should be doing something else persists in your mind.

- **Void** – you will feel somewhat empty on the inside and nothing will satisfy you.

- **Isolation** – you find yourself not wishing to be bothered by anyone; you may be in the presence of other people but constantly feeling as though you need to break away.

- **Confusion in the Mind** – you find yourself in a state of constant confusion while excessive thoughts bombard your mind continually

HOW TO OVERCOME SPIRITUAL FRUSTRATION

Some of the major factors which contribute to many people experiencing spiritual frustration is the fact that either their prayer life, times of worship and studying the Word, or their service to God has been greatly challenged.

Whenever you do not pray or spend much needed time with God, this begins to weaken you spiritually, making you vulnerable to the enemy. You must do everything you can to get rid of spiritual frustration.

Therefore, whenever you begin to feel any level of spiritual frustration you must seek to fortify your relationship with God by:

- Breaking away from your daily routine and finding somewhere to go before Him

- Building a prayer altar

- Immerse yourself in the Word of God and Worship

- Allowing yourself to pour out your heart to God and tell Him exactly how you feel

- Asking Holy Spirit to help you

- Seeking guidance or counsel from your spiritual leader or someone that is seasoned in the things of God. You must trust your spiritual leader from whom you are seeking help

- Remaining willing to obey or adhere to every godly instruction throughout the entire process of your deliverance.

It is not the will of God that you should be spiritually frustrated. This debilitating condition can hinder your progress in the things of God. You must aggressively seek out your deliverance and learn how to maintain it. One of the first steps towards your deliverance is adhering to the principles outlined in the **12 Days Prayer Routine** in this book.

WHY SOME PRAYERS ARE NOT ANSWERED

For the most part, it would seem as though prayer is one of the last things on the daily agenda of some people. Over the years it has been proven that prayer meetings are one of the least attended services at some churches.

At times people can become more consumed with the affairs and cares of life than with prayer. Many people abandon prayer and do not take the time to tap into the power that they have, through prayer, as a believer. Also, many are not prepared to pray persistently until their victory is won.

As a result, many believers are not experiencing the levels of success they can attain through prayer. This lack of success fosters a tendency for them to begin to ascribe to the things of the world more than the things of God

I also believe the enemy knows that one of the greatest weapons that God has given the Body of Christ is prayer. I further believe that many believers are challenged in the area of prayer because the enemy hinders them during these times in an effort to keep the believer spiritually malnourished.

The enemy seeks to utilize or manipulate various barriers in order to seek to hinder and even sabotage some of your prayers. You must continually pray and ask God to help you overcome every barrier to your prayers.

BARRIERS TO YOUR PRAYER

There are **barriers** or **hindrances** which serve as obstacles to your prayers. These barriers seek to block you from entering the throne room of God.

These hindrances may include:
- Your flesh (or your unrejuvenated mind)
- The opinions of others.
- Your surrounding conditions or *atmospheric climate.*
- The second heaven, which is the kingdom of darkness where satan & demonic entities dwell.

A fully developed prayer life produces spiritual power to overcome every attack of the enemy. If you do not fight to develop your prayer times, you will become vulnerable and overwhelmed by the enemy.

Most people become frustrated and ready to give up, simply because they ignored Holy Spirit and the call to pray; to their detriment. Here are a few reasons why some people do not pray and why some people's prayers are not answered:

1) **Carnality:** Christians who are considered to be carnal are more controlled by their fleshly desires than they are led by the Spirit of God. These people generally entertain sin in their life. They prefer activities which may enhance sensual desires or things which satisfy their personal desires rather than doing the will of God or pleasing the spirit of God. For the most part, their hearts are less sensitive to the things of God and more adaptable to this world's system. They have more confidence in the things of the world than the principles and practices of the Kingdom of God .

2) **Lack of perseverance:** In this *instant society* in which we live many people are not prepared to persevere long enough in prayer to obtain their desired results. In some instances, they become impatient and tend to give up too quickly right at the brink of their breakthrough, not realizing that the enemy has assigned demonic principalities to rule over certain areas to hinder their prayers. In Daniel 3 the demonic prince that ruled over Persia withstood Daniel's prayer for over 21 days no. Although his answer was delayed, Daniel continued in prayer during those 21 days. His persistence caught the attention of heaven which employed angels to fight on his behalf, releasing his answer to

him. As a believer, you must be prepared to persevere until you experience your breakthrough.

3) **_Lack of consistency:_**   Some people are not patient or disciplined enough to wait on God or for the results of their prayer to manifest.   At times, many opt to pray once or twice concerning a matter but, when the results do not manifest quickly, they generally seek other solutions to their dilemma. **_Matthew 7:7_** reveals that believers are encouraged to ask, seek and knock until doors are opened and answers are received. These acts imply a consistent or persistent attitude towards prayer.

4) **_Lack of focus:_**   In order to pray effectively, your prayer must have a focus and a direction. Many people do not focus or target their prayers. They are praying foolishly and without direction. This is why, as a Prayer Coach, I encourage individuals to write a prayer resume that will outline the objective or desired outcome of their prayer.   This helps them to persist in their efforts, dispel distractions and focus on praying prayers that bring results.

5) **_Praying amiss_**:   Sometimes when people pray they do not see the manifestation of their prayer because they are praying amiss; as stated in the Bible. These are prayers that are prayed with the wrong motives. When Jesus taught His disciples to pray in **_Luke 11_**, He told them to pray that the will of God would be done on earth as it is in heaven. The prayers of the righteous are intended to enact the will of God in the earth realm, not to fulfill

sensual or carnal desires. Going before God with **self-promoting** prayers sometimes result in these prayers going unanswered, and may cause the believer to become discouraged. You must maintain the right attitude towards prayer and belief in prayer, knowing that as you pray with the right motive, God will answer you.

6) ***Too busy to pray:*** The Word of God admonishes us that we are not to be entangled in the affairs of this life and that ***any man that warreth***, through prayer, will not become consumed with carnal matters. Many times our focus in life becomes impressing our boss, climbing the *corporate ladder* or making another dollar. Some people seem to be more willing to work on building their personal careers than gaining a spiritual promotion in the Kingdom of God. The Word of God warns us that no man can serve two masters; either he will hate one and love the other or despise one and cling to the other. No man can serve God and this world's system equally. At times, many people take on a "Martha" spirit of busyness when they should be more yielded to God in a time of prayer ***(Luke 10:40-42).*** You should never allow yourself to become so busy that you begin to compromise your times in prayer. These precious moments help to cultivate an intimate relationship with God and should always be first priority.

7) ***Too lazy or tired to pray:*** Being too lazy or too tired to pray has a direct correlation with being too busy to pray. If you overwork yourself, you will become tired. However, you should never allow yourself to get to the point where you are so tired that you cannot pray. I believe that when you begin to see prayer as vitally important you will begin to schedule, and remain faithful to, your times of prayer. **In *Matthew 26:40*** Jesus asked His disciples, ***"Can you not watch and pray with me one hour?"*** But they were too tired to stay awake and pray with Jesus. He told them that it was necessary for them to pray so that they would not succumb to the temptations of the enemy. He also told them that He realized that their spirit was willing but the flesh was weak.

Prayer is work. It does require effort and there are many times we do not exert the necessary energy, in prayer, in order to break through to your victory. Again how willing or desperate are you? You must do whatever it takes to build yourself up in prayer. When it comes to prayer, you must command your spirit man to override your carnal man. You must put your flesh under subjection because your flesh naturally resists prayer.

In *Luke 18:1* Jesus instructs His disciples that ***men ought always to pray and not faint.*** The need to pray must override how you feel. Busyness or tiredness should never be used as an excuse to neglect your times of prayer. In The Garden of Gethsemane Jesus was no doubt very tired. He had just preached the gospel, cast out demons and healed the sick, yet he pushed beyond

His weariness and prayed because of the enormity of what He knew He would be facing. How desperate and determined are you for a breakthrough?

HOW THE PYTHON SPIRIT CAUSES PRAYERLESSNESS

Many people struggle and do not have a strong prayer life because of the Python Spirit. In fact, I have noticed that many people have a great social life, but consistently maintain a very weak, even non-existent prayer life.

The spirit of the python causes prayerlessness. This demonic spirit strikes in an effort to bring heaviness and death. It is that spirit which constricts, restricts and tries to manipulate you from praying. It causes tiredness and sleepiness during your times of prayer or study in the Word of God. You may become drowsy or distracted and may even experience extreme fatigue and weariness. This spirit works with the *spirit of divination* and convinces you that you can always pray another day or at some other time.

Divination is foretelling by occultic; dark, hidden or secret, means. The Greek word for Divination is Python. This spirit wraps itself around people's minds. It uses falsehood and fallacies to speak lies into their thoughts about the things of God while exalting its own powers.

This is why some people prefer to receive a prophecy more than prayer. Although prophecy is good, prayer is always better. In fact prayer should always precede prophecy. The Python spirit always tries to suffocate and may even try to choke your desire to pray.

You may sometimes feel as though something is wrapped around your neck during prayer time. Most people have difficulty in speaking and may start coughing or literally begin to strangle.

The spirit of the python may also cause you to be overtaken by cares of life or busy with other things such as: work, school, social events, community service, political efforts and more. Whereas all of these may be good nothing should ever replace your prayer life or time spent in the presence of God.

Whenever *the spirit of divination* is attacking a church it works to eliminate prayer sessions and encourage more social events. These churches have sleepovers, cook outs, fashion shows and prefer workshops or mainstream motivational sessions instead of prayer services.

The leadership unknowingly makes excuses for not having prayer at church. They say things like they do not want to bother the people too much. They de-emphasize prayer and tell everyone to pray whenever or wherever they have a chance. This should not be. The spirit of God emphasized in *Isaiah 56:7* and again in *Matthew 21:13* that His house should be known as a House of Prayer. The Breaker's Anointing is needed to defeat the Spirit of the Python in your personal life and ministry.

ALL PRAYER IS NOT PRAYER

Have you ever been to a place in your life where you felt as if your back was against the wall and there was nowhere to turn? You constantly give of yourself to others and now when you have a need, there is no one there for you?

Maybe on your routine visit to your doctor you received devastating news regarding your health that almost paralyzed you. Perhaps your once picture perfect, story book marriage is not just on the rocks but hanging over the proverbial cliff. If that was not enough, your child is acting out and being labeled by the school system as a menace to society. To add insult to injury, financial crises have invaded your life.

Your heart deeply aches and there is nothing left for you to do but rely on divine, supernatural intervention from God and pray. So you enter your *secret place* and begin crying and complaining, merely talking about your problems rather than praying about them in order to reach a resolution.

All prayer is not prayer. Far too often many people are guilty of praying their problems rather than seeking God for a solution. They have not mastered the art of praying *through* their problems. God is not moved by your constant complaining or murmuring. Neither is He moved by your doubt or inconsistency.

Rather, He is moved by your sincere brokenness and humility. He is moved by His Word and your faith. When you come before His presence and simply rehearse the problem you have not yet prayed. Therefore, in order for you to engage in effective prayer you will need to create what I call *your personal prayer resume.*

YOUR PERSONAL PRAYER RESUME

In order for you to experience the desired outcome of interacting with God there are some factors you should incorporate to help you shape or define your prayer.

As you outline your natural goals and dreams, you may have to prepare a resume, business plan or business proposal, as you chart a course to effect change in your life. Likewise, you must also seek to develop a strategy or personal prayer resume uniquely designed to unlock supernatural miracles on your behalf.

Your Prayer Mission Statement

As you begin to establish a consistent prayer routine, I suggest that you define a prayer mission statement. This guides you in *setting a watch against your enemy.*

Setting a watch against the enemy involves consecrating a pre-determined time each day that you go before God concerning a specific matter. It is similar to assigning a security officer to stand guard and monitor activity going in and coming out. Similarly, as a sentry is assigned to stand watch in the Armed Forces at a focal point, such as a gate, even so, you must be positioned and spiritually armed to watch, in prayer, against your enemy.

"I will stand upon my watch, and set me upon the tower, and will watch to see what he will say unto me, and what I shall answer when I am reproved." **(Habbakuk 2:1)**

41 Watch and pray, that ye enter not into temptation: the spirit indeed is willing, but the flesh is weak. (Matthew 26:41)

Jesus told His disciples in **Matthew 26:41** to watch, or stay alert and pray. Further, you can set a watch as an individual or with the assistance of others. Your sacrifice of committing to pray at the same time every day sends a message in the realm of the spirit that you are trying to capture God's attention in this urgent matter.

For example, if one of your prayer goals is to dethrone the spirit of poverty and lack in your life, you may establish a prayer mission statement that you will pray every day at **12 noon and 12 midnight** to reverse this diabolical curse of the enemy. There are other spiritual weapons you may employ to intensify your attack against the enemy such as fasting, sowing, reading the Word and others.

PLANNING YOUR PERSONAL PRAYER TIME

Every time you pray your prayer should have a purpose, aim, objective or conclusion. Your primary reason for initiating a conversation with God is that you are expecting Him to send the answer to your dilemma or send divine intervention.

As you pursue your breakthrough in the realm of the spirit your prayer resume can be outlined with a *definite purpose, aim, objective, and conclusion.*

- The **Purpose** of your prayer defines the reason why you are petitioning God for an answer or divine intervention. *For example, You may pray, "Lord I need you because..."*

- The **Aim** of your prayer is the focus that you will take as you approach the throne room of God and what will also determine the type of prayer you will pray. Further, the aim identifies your intended target. *For example, you can begin praying the prayer of faith because you need God to heal you.*

- The **Objective** of your prayer is the defined outcome and result of your prayer. Further, the objective of your prayer also explains your expectation or desired outcome. *For example, your expectation is that God will heal you. When your healing manifests you will know that God heard you and your prayer was effective.*

- The **Conclusion** of your prayer includes giving God the glory for sending the answer and your declaration of victory until your miracle manifests in the natural.

God wants you to continually strengthen yourself spiritually so that you will be equipped to overcome any attack the enemy launches against your life. A fully developed prayer life is one of the greatest weapons against the enemy. Your lifestyle of prayer will open heaven over you.

During times of spiritual warfare the power of prevailing prayer will summon angels to wage war against the enemy on your behalf.

CHAPTER FOUR

THE POWER OF PREVAILING PRAYER

PRAYERS THAT AVAIL
"The effectual fervent prayer of a righteous man availeth much." (James 5:16b)

According to **James 5:16** the Word of God reveals that our fervent, passionate prayers will have an impact here on earth. Also, as mentioned earlier, your prayers should have a specific target with anticipated results. Once your desired expectation is realized, it can be concluded that your prayer was effective. To advance as a sharp shooter in the realm of the spirit you must be prepared to pray earnest, militant, targeted prayers. ***Here are a few secrets to praying effective, prevailing prayer:***

- You must identify and focus on your target. Define your specific needs which warrant prayer and declare scriptures relevant to them.

- Use the spirit of discernment to help you determine how you should pray for them and in which type of prayer to engage.

- Take your aim in the realm of the spirit, declaring God's Word, using the names of God and speaking specifically to the fulfillment of those needs.

- Pronounce destruction to the enemy's plans.

- Continuously give God thanks, glory and honor for the victory in every situation.

Prayer is one of the most powerful weapons given to believers. Over the years I have seen the power of prayer bring healing and deliverance to the lives of many individuals. Yet in many churches prayer meetings are the least attended services. Also, many people do not pray at home. On the contrary, although faced with extreme dilemmas, many continue to sleep through the night without making any effort to set a watch, in prayer, against their enemy.

In order to gain more power to overcome the attacks of the enemy, you must begin to cultivate a consistent prayer life. As you commit to developing a lifestyle of prayer you will begin to cultivate *a spirit of prayer* that will empower you to gain the victory in every area of your life.

THE SPIRIT OF PRAYER

6 Then he answered and spake unto me, saying, This is the word of the LORD unto Zerubbabel, saying, Not by might, nor by power, but by my spirit, saith the LORD of hosts. (Zechariah 4:6)

The spirit of a thing carries the nature or characteristic of that thing. The spirit of a thing is what governs and literally drives *it* to become what *it* truly is. Therefore, when you carry the spirit of prayer you are literally carrying the truest essence of prayer.

Every believer needs to be endowed with *the spirit of prayer*. The spirit of prayer is attained in the life of a believer who is committed to making prayer his lifestyle. Whenever you practice or habitually do something, you begin to develop a propensity for that thing.

When you have the spirit of prayer, prayer becomes a natural or normal part of your character and you develop an innate ability to pray. Prayer becomes you and you become prayer, which means that prayer becomes intricately and intimately interwoven in your spirit and you find it easy to pray about everything. Prayer happens spontaneously where you find yourself talking to God almost involuntarily. You will know that you have developed a spirit of prayer when prayer is at the forefront of everything that you do.

MANTLED WITH THE SPIRIT OF PRAYER

Anyone can become mantled to pray once they commit to spending quality time in the presence of God. Just as you can physically see what someone is wearing in the natural, through spiritual discernment you can always perceive when someone is carrying the mantle of prayer.

When you are mantled with a spirit of prayer you automatically become a prayer carrier and you begin to *wear prayer* like a garment.

This means that you carry the fragrance of prayer and the ability to effect positive change, through prayer, everywhere you go. This fragrance represents the anointing. The anointing to pray is what removes the burden and destroys every yoke of the enemy. The Bible states,

> *"...that his burden shall be taken away from off thy shoulder, and his yoke from off thy neck, and the yoke shall be destroyed because of the anointing." (Isaiah 10:27)*

A *prayer carrier* is someone who is mantled with an anointing to pray. As a prayer carrier you pray always and everywhere. You carry the burden to pray in your spirit all the way to the prayer altar.

> *13 And said unto them, It is written, My house*
> *shall be called the house of prayer;*
> *(Matthew 21:13)*

Jesus reiterated what the prophet Isaiah declared years ago in **Isaiah 56:7**; the house of the Lord would be called, or better, known as, *the gathering place,* the place where prayers get results.

However, what we have seen over the years was everything but prayers and very few results. It almost seemed as though most churches have lost the spirit of prayer and are now settling with merely becoming a social meeting place, promoting everything from fashion shows to pajamas night. The Spirit of God is calling the church back to its first calling – prayer.

Being mantled as a prayer carrier does not exempt you from attending church or assembling with other saints. In addition to your corporate worship, you can develop your prayer life to the degree that you erect temporary prayer altars everywhere and touch heaven.

A spiritual prayer altar can be built in the privacy of your home. However, as a prayer carrier, you should also embrace the opportunity to use the sacred altar that is in your local church. The unction to pray moves with you to call on God at any time, in any place and anywhere; because you are the temple of Holy Ghost.

¹ O God, thou art my God; early will I seek thee: my soul thirsteth for thee, my flesh longeth for thee in a dry and thirsty land, where no water is;

² To see thy power and thy glory, so as I have seen thee in the sanctuary. (Psalm 63:1- 2)

BUILDING A SPIRITUAL ALTAR

When I speak of building a spiritual altar, I am referring to a place or area that has been consecrated and set apart for you to pray and seek the face of God.

This can be a specific area in your home such as a closet that you have set aside and deemed holy unto the Lord. Some people may even use a bathroom or a portion of your living room. Whatever place you choose to dedicate for the purpose of seeking the face of God, that place can be called your *personal spiritual altar.*

My personal altar was a space in my closet where I had set up several shoe boxes and covered them with a prayer cloth. I kept a Bible, notepad, pen, highlighter, a box of Kleenex, a small bottle oil and a small bottle of drinking water in that area. I wanted to be ready at all times should Holy Spirit lead me in a time of prayer or wanted to speak to me. I kept everything in that small area.

My walls were always covered with scriptures, prayer points and some of the things for which I was praying. This was my personal altar and from that place I fought many battles and obtained great victories.

Throughout the Old Testament you will see where many mighty men and women of God, such as David, built a memorial or used a threshing floor as a sacred place to seek God.

Thirsty, Desperate Prayer Warriors

As the Psalmist declared, he longed to see the glory of God and to experience the presence of God as he had seen it manifest during times of worship in the Temple **(Psalm63:2).** As a prayer carrier, what you do in your private times of worship produces a desperate desire to pray everywhere. I found myself praying compulsively, whether in the grocery store or the mall, because I was sensitive to Holy Spirit. *Prayer became normal for me.*

The Children of Israel wandered through the wilderness for a long time. They had no physical home or place of worship except the Tabernacle which God had given to Moses. This tent they carried wherever they went was the place where God came down to commune and tabernacle with them.

God later gave King David the blueprint for the Temple. This would become the physical building where God would meet His people and they would bring sacrifices and offer them up to God. Although David was given the blueprint, God anointed David's son, Solomon, to build His holy temple.

Today God desires to more closely tabernacle with His people. His desire for spiritual intimacy transcends a physical building as He now desires a place in the heart and life of every believer.

Your body now serves as the Temple of the Holy Ghost where God directly tabernacles with you and prayer can now be constant and consistent. It is His ultimate desire that we become intimate with Him and commune with Him through prayer.

ACTIVATING THE SPIRIT OF PRAYER

Once the spirit of prayer is activated in your life you will find yourself manifesting in prayer at any given time. You do not have to be prompted to pray. You do not have to force yourself to pray, it happens supernaturally. Prayer, like the Word of God, becomes your two-edged sword which erupts out of your spirit as you are inspired by the Spirit of God.

Prayer becomes a normal response or reaction to every situation you are facing. No matter how tragic, devastating or life-altering the issue is or appears to be, prayer becomes automatically evoked from your spirit. When you have been activated with the spirit of prayer, you become endowed with a supernatural ability to pray at any given moment, gaining your victory.

Prophetically, your entire life will change as the spirit of prayer causes many great things to happen:

- **The spirit of prayer** will cause you to pray through every aisle at the grocery store. You may have a small, or what I call a $50-budget but, as you pray; God will give you supernatural wisdom that will cause your monies to yield more than you had anticipated.

- **The spirit of prayer** will cause you to pray your child's team to victory while you are sitting in the bleachers. As you are in the stands, dispatch the angel of the Lord to the field to help your child catch every ball and accurately swing every time at bat.

- **The spirit of prayer** will cause you to pray your family back to health regardless of what is attacking them.

- **The spirit of prayer** will cause you to change the loan officer's decline of your credit application into an approval.

- **The spirit of prayer** produces a fragrance that attracts the presence of God to your life.

- **The spirit of prayer** will cause you to win contracts when you are not even eligible for them.

- **The spirit of prayer** causes supernatural doors to open and demonic doors to shut.

> *The Spirit of Prayer Will Cause Nothing To Be Impossible To You!*

Further, you will know that you have the spirit of prayer when:

- You are filled with the compassion to pray for others.
- You cannot help but pray. You constantly have prophetic geysers. ***(See more in my book "I STILL WANT YOU–The Call To A Deeper Place")***
- Your passion for prayer supersedes everything else.
- You awake in the middle of the night and you automatically begin to pray.
- You carry the fragrance of prayer.
- You carry the language and speech of prayer.
- You see prayer as the solution to every problem.
- You have uncommon favor everywhere you go.
- You have good success in every area of your life.
- You develop a keen sense of discernment as your spiritual senses are heightened; more and more you begin to see things the way God sees them.
- You find it easy to forgive and love others.
- You find joy in serving God and fulfilling your kingdom assignment.
- You look forward to your prayer times and being in the presence of God.
- You instinctively employ the weapon of prayer when confronted by the enemy.
- You experience supernatural events regularly.
- Miracles become common and a part of your daily life.
- You embrace every opportunity to be used by God.

LACKING THE SPIRIT OF PRAYER

You can always identify someone who is carrying the spirit of prayer. Likewise, you can easily tell when someone **does not** have the spirit of prayer. These people are generally very carnal, critical or chronic complainers. They are idle, busybodies who are very negative and often exacerbate the problem.

They generally tend to see the problem bigger than the solution and prefer to talk about a problem rather than identifying ways to fix it. On the other hand, when they do talk about solutions it is usually done so in a critical or demeaning manner.

> *When you are void of the spirit of prayer in your life, the enemy seeks every opportunity to weaken you and sabotage your miracles.*

Even when you attempt to pray, if you do not have the spirit of prayer you may find that you:
- Constantly fall asleep
- Complain often and frequently make excuses
- Pray amiss or with insincere motives and unbelief
- Become easily distracted or run short of words
- Continuously fall into sin
- Are unable to easily love or forgive others
- Have difficulty reading your Bible or witnessing to others

- Become more susceptible to the attacks of the enemy
- Become stuck in demonic cycles repeating the same thing making the same mistakes
- Constantly battle generational and other curses in your life

The Spirit of Prayer Must Be Cultivated

Everywhere you look it would seem as though the enemy has intensified his warfare tactics. If you are going to continue to experience any level of victory in your walk with God you will have to cultivate the spirit of prayer in your life.

*This cultivation will involve reconditioning your flesh from **not** wanting to pray; to preparing your spirit to pray every day.* The general purpose for spiritual cultivation to develop the spirit of prayer is so that you produce a harvest of great things in your life and the lives of countless others.

Once the spirit of prayer is cultivated and you begin to prosper in life, this will eventually lead to you developing a *spirit of intercession.*

THE SPIRIT OF INTERCESSION

[26]Likewise the Spirit also helpeth our inifirmities: or we know not what we should pray for as we ought: but the Spirit itself maketh intercession for us with groaning which cannot be uttered.

12 MINUTES TO BREAKTHROUGH

*²⁷And he that searcheth the hearts knoweth
what is the mind of the Spirit because he
maketh intercession for the saints according to
the will of God. (Romans 8:26, 27)*

Intercession is a consistent or persistent prayer made on behalf of someone else until their victory manifests. As you consistently pray, Holy Spirit becomes your Teacher, Guide, Comforter and Intercessor.

As you seek Him He fills you with the spirit of intercession, causing you to pray and bear someone else's burden. Bearing another's burden does not mean that you become stressed or overwhelmed, it means you become passionate about their situation.

At times the spirit of prayer will cause you to pray when you are not even naturally conscious of why you are praying. Whenever this begins to happen it can mean that your prayer life has elevated to the point where you are now moving in the spirit of intercession.

The Greek word for intercession is *"Pagha"*, which means to strike upon or against. To intercede means to go between two litigants. *Inter* is a prefix meaning *among* or *between*; *cede* or *cess* is a Latin root word meaning *forego, yield or surrender.*

In other words, as an intercessor you stand between the problem and the solution, making the problem submit to the Word and will of God. Some weapons which demonstrate the type of intercessory prayer of striking are: *the hammer, the fire, the wrecking ball, the battering ram and others.*

THE INTERCEDING PROPHET

The spirit of intercession is the spirit of Elijah. It represents those who are mantled with an anointing to pray beyond the barriers of demonic confrontations. Elijah was a mighty prophet of God who called fire down from heaven, not so much because he was a prophet but, more so because he was an intercessor.

I believe that by reason of his prayers or as a result of his continual praying, Elijah had attained a level of spiritual authority which empowered him to instruct heaven and command the elements to obey his prophetic voice.

Although Elijah was a prophet, he spent much time in prayer and intercession. Many times people make the terrible mistake of spending more time trying to become a prophet or wanting the gift of prophecy rather than spending time in prayer.

> *[17] Elias was a man subject to like passions as we are, and he prayed earnestly that it might not rain: and it rained not on the earth by the space of three years and six months.*
> *(James 5:17)*

The Word of God reveals that Elijah was a man with passions and desires like any other man or woman. However, Elijah knew how to shift the atmosphere over an entire region; he knew how to discern the voice of God because he had made prayer his practice.

Your consistency in prayer will create a culture of prayer that, in turn, becomes a lifestyle. In the realm of the spirit, the Word of God teaches that you eventually become a servant to whatever you yield yourself.

> [13] *"Neither yield ye your members as instruments of unrighteousness unto sin: but yield yourselves unto God,..."*
> *(Romans 6:13)*

To yield means to submit or surrender your will. Rather than yielding your members to sin, you can yield your members to the obedience of the Spirit of God. This leads to *righteousness* as defined by God's Word.

As you yield yourself to the times when He is calling you to pray, you will soon attract the spirit of prayer to your life. However, if you continue to ignore these times of prayer then the burden to pray as prompted the Holy Spirit will begin to diminish.

God wants to demonstrate His power to His people in greater dimensions. When you cultivate the spirit of prayer or intercession you invite the presence of God to intervene in your life, activating supernatural miracles and unexpected breakthroughs.

SPIRITUAL LEGAL RIGHTS

Every believer has the legal right to enter the throne room of God. As an intercessor you become the mediator and you are mandated to carry spiritual burdens which may include the burden of a family, a group of friends, an entire community, a country or even a social cause. In other words, you take on the assignment to pray *for* and to pray *with* someone until there is absolute change.

Similar to the functions a lawyer performs, you take burdens to the court of heaven praying and legally advocating on behalf of others until the victory is won. Whenever lawyers go to court regarding any matter they lean on the laws which govern that jurisdiction. You must lean on kingdom laws in order to experience similar victories.

In order to benefit as a citizen of the Kingdom of God, you must know your legal rights and how to enact them. If you do not understand what you are legally entitled to, you will remain bound by your adversary. The blood of Jesus Christ gives you all legal rights to be free from bondage and demonic attacks. You give over your legal rights to the enemy when you allow sin to reign in your life.

Strive to heed the voice of God by obeying His Word. This will keep you legally protected. *(Read Romans 8:2)*

OPERATING IN DIVINE AUTHORITY

As a believer, it is important that you understand spiritual or divine authority and why you must exercise it. Authority is having the right or power to give orders and instructions, expecting them to be carried out. You have already received delegated authority to bind every evil spirit through the power of the blood of Jesus Christ.

Verily I say unto you, Whatsoever ye shall bind on earth shall be bound in heaven: and whatsoever ye shall loose on earth shall be loosed in heaven. (Matthew 18:18).

When you speak or pray with authority the devil has to leave in Jesus name. Speaking with authority is speaking with boldness and confidence. It is to fearlessly declare victory over the kingdom of darkness, commanding the enemy's defeat. When you know your authority in God you will begin to breakthrough beyond all barriers.

THE COURTS OF HEAVEN

"Bless ye the Lord, All ye servants of the Lord, which by night stand in the courts of the Lord" (Psalm 134:1)

Just as there are courts on earth there are courts in the realm of the spirit. There are courts in the kingdom of darkness and there are courts in the kingdom of Heaven. The courts of the Lord have been established to plead the cases of the people of God. It is the blood of Jesus Christ that gives you divine access to the courts of heaven.

3 Blessed be the God and Father of our Lord Jesus Christ, who hath blessed us with all spiritual blessings in heavenly places in Christ:

4 According as he hath chosen us in him before the foundation of the world, that we should be holy and without blame before him in love:

5 Having predestinated us unto the adoption of children by Jesus Christ to himself, according to the good pleasure of his will,

⁶ To the praise of the glory of his grace, wherein he hath made us accepted in the beloved.

⁷ In whom we have redemption through his blood, the forgiveness of sins, according to the riches of his grace;
(Ephesians 1:3–7)

Every believer will have absolute victory in the courts of heaven as we embrace the grace of God available to us through Jesus' shed blood. Grace is not a thing but Grace is Jesus, Himself. It is the grace of God that vindicates you. Grace means that you are not deserving of something but it is extended to you nonetheless.

⁸ For by grace are ye saved through faith; and that not of yourselves: it is the gift of God:

⁹ Not of works, lest any man should boast.
(Ephesians 2:8–9)

When you become fully persuaded and accept grace as your ticket for the rights of passage in the spirit real, then you will experience breakthrough at every stage of your life.

THE ACCUSER

Satan is the accuser of the brethren and he constantly seeks opportunities to bring railing accusations against the righteous, as seen in **Zechariah 3:1–2** with Joshua, the high priest.

¹And he shewed me Joshua the high priest standing before the angel of the LORD, and Satan standing at his right hand to resist him.

² And the LORD said unto Satan, The LORD rebuke thee, O Satan; even the LORD that hath chosen Jerusalem rebuke thee: is not this a brand plucked out of the fire?

Every court system has such rules and regulations which govern it. So is the case with the courts of the Lord. As you pray earnestly your prayers are taken before the courts of the Lord. The Spirit of God then takes those prayers and makes intercession for you with groans that cannot be uttered, seeking only favorable results.

²⁶ Likewise the Spirit also helpeth our infirmities: for we know not what we should pray for as we ought: but the Spirit itself maketh intercession for us with groanings which cannot be uttered.

²⁷ And he that searcheth the hearts knoweth what is the mind of the Spirit, because he maketh intercession for the saints according to the will of God. (Romans 8:26, 27)

As you earnestly offer up prayer in the spirit before the Lord, your *guilty* verdict changes to *not guilty*. Your charges are dropped and all condemnation against you is removed. You become fully exonerated, all of your records are wiped clean and you are esteemed as though you never had a case. Practice taking your request to the courts of heaven and watch God divinely give you the victory every time.

There is therefore now no condemnation to them which are in Christ Jesus, who walk not after the flesh, but after the Spirit. (Romans 8:1)

When God completely vindicates you and expunges your records it is documented throughout eternity and every spirit of condemnation is broken from over your life.

YOUR DIVINE COVENANT

17 And if children, then heirs; heirs of God, and joint-heirs with Christ; if so be that we suffer with him, that we may be also glorified together. (Romans 8:17)

Once you accept the gift of salvation in the name of Jesus you are saved, and you have been engrafted into the Kingdom of God through the blood of Jesus Christ. As a Kingdom citizen you are, therefore, entitled to every benefit as outlined in the divine constitution called the Bible.

6 And hath raised us up together, and made us sit together in heavenly places in Christ Jesus: (Ephesians 2:6)

In **Ephesians 2:6** the Bible reveals that we are seated with Christ in heavenly places. This means that the same benefits that Jesus received we are entitled to. Prayer is the prophetic key that unlocks the door to supernatural miracles. Activate your divine covenant and watch God answer your prayers.

CHAPTER FIVE

GOD ANSWERS PRAYER

GOD ANSWERS PRAYER

Many people in the Body of Christ are defeated in their efforts because they are unable to discern when God has sent the answer to their dilemma. At times they are looking for God to come a certain way and may miss a divine opportunity because it does not look or sound like God.

> *[11] And he said, Go forth, and stand upon the mount before the LORD. And, behold, the LORD passed by, and a great and strong wind rent the mountains, and brake in pieces the rocks before the LORD;* but *the LORD was not in the wind: and after the wind an earthquake; but the LORD was not in the earthquake:*
>
> *[12] And after the earthquake a fire; but the LORD was not in the fire: and after the fire a still small voice. (1 Kings 19:11, 12)*

The prophet Elijah had seen God move in many different ways. He saw the Spirit of God manifesting in the form of a strong wind, earthquake, fire and the like. However, in **1 Kings 19:12** God did not reveal Himself to the prophet in any of the ways which He had previously done. This time God chose to manifest himself in the form of a still small voice.

If the prophet was moved by his emotions or was prone to reason everything through in his mind, He may have believed God was speaking to him through the ways in which God had before spoken to him. However, he considered the signs and discerned the voice of God because he had developed a relationship with God through prayer. Spiritual sensitivity is very important to your total victory.

Whenever prayer becomes your priority you will discern the ways God answers you. As a prophetic intercessor you can elevate to a realm of spiritual intimacy with God where you know the phenomenal, multifaceted ways of God and not only His acts.

> *7 He made known his ways unto Moses, his acts unto the children of Israel. (Psalm 103:7)*

God generally sends the answer to your prayer from three different realms. *He can answer your prayer from The Realm of His Sovereign Will, The Realm of Angels or The Realm of Human Will.*

1) **When God answers you from The Realm of God's Sovereign Will** God Himself shows up and divinely intervenes and answers your prayer.

> *6 And I will add to your days fifteen years. I will deliver you and this city from the hand of the king of Assyria; and I will defend this city for My own sake, and for the sake of My servant David.*

For example, in *2 Kings 20:6* God answered King Hezekiah and changed the judgment of death on his life after the Prophet Isaiah had declared that he was going to die. God, Himself, intervened and added *15 more years* to Hezekiah's life.

In *Exodus 33* God spoke directly to Moses and placed him in the cleft of the rock while His Glory passed by.

This was a prayer answered for Moses. He longed to see the glory of God and God answered him. As you pray earnestly, God will, at times, speak directly to you. That is what I call the sovereign move of God.

2) When God answers you from the Realm of Angels or from The Supernatural Realm He dispatches angels to bring answers to your prayers. For example, in ***Daniel 10*** an angel is sent from the throne room of God to give Daniel the answer to his prayer.

> *¹¹ And he said unto me, O Daniel, a man greatly beloved, understand the words that I speak unto thee, and stand upright: for unto thee am I now sent. And when he had spoken this word unto me, I stood trembling.*

> *¹² Then said he unto me, Fear not, Daniel: for from the first day that thou didst set thine heart to understand, and to chasten thyself before thy God, thy words were heard, and I am come for thy words. (Daniel 10:11, 12)*

As you pray earnestly your prayer of faith will activate the supernatural realm of God. God will then dispatch His angels to work on your behalf.

> *Angels of God Do Not Interfere, They Intervene*

3) When God answers you from the Realm of Human Will God will speak to the heart of a human being to bless you. However, the human being that He is using has to choose to obey the voice of God. For example, Adam was given the power to obey God or to obey his own thoughts. God spoke to the prophet Jonah to go and preach the gospel to the people of Nineveh but Jonah decided to go the opposite way. After a series of dilemmas occurred in Jonah's life, he ended up in Nineveh and preached to the people who eventually received the gospel and obtained salvation.

The human will influences what a person decides to do. God can speak to someone. However, a person's obedience is predicated on his free will and willingness to obey the Spirit of God. This is the realm of human will.

¹And the word of the LORD came unto Jonah the second time, saying,

²Arise, go unto Nineveh, that great city, and preach unto it the preaching that I bid thee.

³So Jonah arose, and went unto Nineveh, according to the word of the LORD.
(Jonah 3:1–3a)

Reluctantly, Jonah eventually aligned his will with the will of God and through this human vessel the people of Nineveh were set free by the power of God. As a believer, in your desperation, sometimes you may need to resort to radical measures to get answers to your prayer.

PILLARS AND ATTRIBUTES OF PRAYER

As you continue in prayer have faith and trust that God still answers prayer. During my times of prayer I discovered what I call over forty attributes, attitudes and characteristics which prepared me to pray more effectively. Adopting these attributes was the key element to getting the desired answer to my prayers.

Just as every believer must possess the *fruit of the Spirit (Galatians 5:22–23)* to live a victorious Christian life, I believe that in order for you to effectively engage in intercession it is necessary that you possess various attributes, behaviors and attitudes towards prayer.

Some of those attributes include, but are not limited to, the following:

- **The Attribute of Active Faith**
  To have faith is to totally trust God and take Him at His Word. The Bible declares that without faith it is impossible to please God **(Hebrews 11:6).** It is also impossible to pray without faith. Faith sees the prayer as answered despite what the situation looks like and says, *"Yes, Lord, I believe!"* God then honors your act of praying in faith and moves on your behalf. **(James 5:13–18)**

- **The Attribute of Having The Power To Believe**
  When you pray and believe, you are fully convinced that God has heard and answered your prayer. Having faith in God and actively believing in God work simultaneously. According to **Hebrews 11:6** you must believe that God is who He says He is: Creator, Redeemer, Provider, King of Kings, Lord of lords, Healer, Deliverer and so much more. Belief in God is the foundation of your prayers. It would be futile to pray to someone who you do not

believe exists or can answer your prayers. You were saved by belief in God according to **Acts 16:31** and **John 3:16**. Now, it takes that same belief to trust Him to answer your prayer.

● **The Attribute of Confidence**

If you are a parent I am sure you have had the experience where your child asks you for something because he knows that you have it. The child asks in confidence, knowing that you will provide it for him. Our Heavenly Father wants you to have that same kind of assurance in Him. He is your Father. The earth and everything in it belongs to Him. Therefore, when we come to God believing Him in confidence and asking anything according to His will, He will grant your request. *(1 John 5:14–15)*

● **The Attribute of Hope**

Hope is the belief that the results or objectives you were praying for will be achieved or obtained. It is fueled by or founded upon your desire to receive something that you are expecting from God. Hope is what sustains you as you wait for the manifestation of your request and it is vital to your success. Hope is the foundation for your faith referred to in **Hebrews 11:1**, *Now faith is the substance of things hoped for, the evidence of things not seen.*

Hope motivates you to believe God, no matter how the situation looks or what may arise. The Word of God reveals, in **Romans 4:18** that against hope Abraham *believed in hope, that he might*

become the father of many nations, according to that which was spoken.

- ### The Attribute of Love

  Agape is the unconditional love of God; you must have the love of God in your heart in order to maintain an effective and consistent prayer life. Having God's unconditional love in your heart compels you to fervently pray for others. *7 Beloved, let us love one another: for love is of God; and every one that loveth is born of God, and knoweth God. 8 He that loveth not knoweth not God; for God is love. (1 John 4:7–8)*

- ### The Attribute of Spiritual Reception

  As a person who is called to prayer you must be open to the leading and counsel of Holy Spirit. The more you draw near to Him in prayer, the more He speaks to you and reveals His divine will. Once you are obedient to the instructions He has given, then He will prosper you. *2 Chronicles 20:20b* states, *"Believe in the Lord your God, so shall ye be established; believe his prophets, so shall ye prosper."*

- ### The Attribute of Obedience

  Obedience means to total compliance with or submission to spiritual instructions. *1 Samuel 15:22* reveals that "to obey is better than sacrifice, and to hearken than the fat of rams." Your complete obedience to the instructions received from Holy Spirit during your times of prayer will determine your level of breakthrough or ultimate victory. *(Joshua 1:8; Deuteronomy 28:1)*

- **The Attributes of Discernment and Sensitivity in the Spirit**
Discernment is a God-given ability to perceive, recognize or ascertain what is happening in the spirit realm. Discerning of spirits is one of the revelatory gifts cultivated by an active prayer life. It causes you to be spiritually sensitive to the will of God.

  This spirit of discernment will cause you to recognize when:
  a) the Spirit of God is in operation and speaking to you.
  b) the spirit of the devil is manifesting.
  c) the human spirit is in control.

  It is most important that you are able to discern the voice of Holy Spirit. In *1 Corinthians 2:14* we are admonished that *the natural man receiveth not the things of the Spirit of God; for they are foolishness unto him; neither can he know them, because they are spiritually discerned.* In your life as a believer discernment is essential, especially during your time of prayer.

- **The Attribute of Persistence**
There is an old adage that says, "If at first you don't succeed, try and try again." Persistence represents a relentless pursuit, steadfast determination and unwavering faith. As a believer, if you are expecting anything from God you do not only pray

once. You must be like the widow in **Luke 18** who persisted until the unjust judge granted her request. On the other hand, God is your loving Father and when you are persistent with your earnest petition He will release the answers to you. *(1 Thessalonians 5:17)*

- **The Attribute of Fervency**

  Have you ever desperately needed God to hear your prayer and been prepared to do whatever it took to get an answer? You might have travailed, paced the floor or even laid prostrate in His presence. Your passion in prayer will attract the presence of God to your situation, just like Hannah in **1 Samuel 1**.

  Your prayer at midnight should be militant. This type of prayer is powerful, fervent, very intense and can reach *the boiling point* **(James 5:16b).** Pray until you get results; pray until you see your breakthrough; pray until your miracle manifests; **P.U.S.H. (Pray Until Something Happens)**

- **The Attribute of Longsuffering**

  According to **Galatians 5:22–23** longsuffering is a fruit of the Spirit. It is also an attribute of prayer that you must possess if you want to achieve results. There are times your answers might be delayed. God heard you when you first prayed and released the answer; however there might be a Prince of Persia trying to block your answer like he tried with Daniel in **Daniel 10:13-21.** You must be willing to persevere in prayer until your breakthrough manifests.

- **The Attribute of Patience**

  Patience and longsuffering work together. If you are to receive anything from God you must be patient, even in prayer. Scripture reminds us that in patience we possess our souls *(Luke 21:19)*. Further, it states that in due season we shall reap if we are patient *(Galatians 6:9)*.

The more attributes of prayer you adopt during your prayer time, the more effective and fervent you will become in prayer. As you begin to adopt more and more of the attributes of prayer transformation will begin to take place and your prayers will become more fervent and more effective.

CHAPTER SIX

PRAYING FOR A
BREAKTHROUGH

TYPES OF PRAYERS FOR BREAKTHROUGH

Throughout the annals of time it has been demonstrated that the men and women of God who have spent quality time seeking God have walked in great power. They adopted prayer as the medium through which they spoke to, communed with and petitioned God to intervene in their personal lives, communities, regions and nations.

The Bible documents the diversity of prayers which vary based on the nature and urgency of the request submitted to God. Some of the types of prayer identified include but are not limited to:

Prayers of Petition

To petition means to make a request, whether informal or formally written. Our petitions are verbal requests made to God during times of prayer. The term **petition** is derived from the Latin word **petere** meaning to claim or ask for. Petitioning is also asking God for the desires of our heart. The Word declares, *"Ask, and it shall be given you..."* **(Matthew 7:7)**. We are commanded to ask.

We can petition God like Jacob who cried out, "I will not let thee go except thou bless me" *(Genesis 32:26)*. We can petition our Father like the widow who petitioned the unjust judge in Luke 18 with consistency and diligence to the point where he said, *"yet because this widow continues to bother me, I will give her justice and legal protection; otherwise by (her) continually coming she [will be an intolerable annoyance and she] will wear me out." (Luke 18:5 AMP)*

Conclusively, Jacob received his blessing and the widow received her request. In faith continue to petition God and He will answer your prayer.

Prayers of Supplication

Supplication means earnestly pleading and entreating God for something. It is a passionate zeal, hunger and fervor which fuels your appeal made in prayer. Jesus wants us to earnestly seek God so that all other things will be supplied in our lives. In **Philippians 4:6** we are encouraged to earnestly seek God by prayer and supplication with thanksgiving.

6 Be careful for nothing; but in every thing by prayer and supplication with thanksgiving let your requests be made known unto God. (Philippians 4:6)

The prayer of supplication is the type of prayer that all Christians should regularly engage in. This is a prayer of desperation where you acknowledge that God is your ultimate source and the solution to all things and you are desperately in need of urgent answers.

Prayers of Repentance

The root word for repentance is repent. To repent means to feel totally sorry for wrong things you have done, to willingly admit your fault, to turn from what you were doing and change your ways. It comes from the old French word which means to feel regret for sins. Repentance is turning away from sin and past wrongs. It speaks to re-direction and commitment to do and live differently.

> *Have mercy upon me, O God, according to thy*
> *loving kindness: according unto the multitude*
> *of thy tender mercies blot out my*
> *transgressions. (Psalms 51:1)*

The Prayer of Repentance is prayed when you are totally sorry for your sins and wrong doings. You pray this prayer unto God when you have acknowledged your short comings and are ready for total change. Repentance means that you are ready to do, different. You are ready for a mind, soul and entire life shift. You no longer want to remain the same. You are so sorry for your sins and short comings. You earnestly desire total change and renewal you become in broken in spirit.

> *The sacrifices of God are a broken spirit: a*
> *broken and a contrite heart, O God, thou wilt*
> *not despise. (Psalms 51:17)*

Godly sorrow is what brings repentance. When you become sorry for your state of being you find yourself moving to repentance. Sincere repentance produces salvation and spiritual elevation.

For godly sorrow worketh repentance to salvation not to be repented of: but the sorrow of the world worketh death.
(2 Corinthians 7:10)

Prayers of Faith

Faith is absolute belief in God and is not based on external factors or circumstances. The Prayer of Faith is founded in our confidence in God's Word. By faith, the woman with the issue of blood knew that touching Jesus would result in her being healed. *(Matthew 9:20–22)*.

According to **James 5:15,** *"And the prayer of faith shall save the sick, and the Lord shall raise him up..."* When you are seeking healing for yourself, or on behalf of others, you must pray in faith.

Therefore I say unto you, What things soever ye desire, when ye pray, believe that ye receive them, and ye shall have them. (Mark 11:24)

Where the Prayer of Supplication appeals to God's will, the prayer of faith denotes that you already know the will of God and can pray with boldness and confidence until you receive the answer.

Prayers of Agreement

In *Matthew 18: 19–20* Jesus said, [19] *"Again I say to you, that if two believers on earth agree [that is, are of one mind, in harmony] about anything that they ask [within the will of God], it will be done for them by My Father in heaven. [20] For where two or three are gathered in My name [meeting together as My followers], I am there among them."*

The Prayer of Agreement is when two or more people come together to pray with a mutual understanding through the Word of God that something specific will be done. They set definite guidelines or a course of conduct for their prayer, anticipating the same results, and are unified as they pray confidently that God will answer them.

The Prayers of Agreement have been proven to get results. As a believer, seek out like-minded people of faith to agree with you on anything; God guarantees that you will get results.

Spiritual Warfare Prayers

Spiritual Warfare is an ensuing battle in the realm of the spirit between the kingdom of God and the kingdom of darkness. It is a perpatual battle that takes place in the invisible realm. In this warfare, we, as believers are already victorious.

Spiritual Warfare Prayers are directed against satan's hierarchy and his demonic principalities, powers, rulers of the darkness of this world and spiritual wickedness in high places *(Ephesians 6:10–12)*. As a believer you will find yourself engaged in some level of warfare with the enemy. It is important that you recognize and learn the nature of the enemy's attack against your life and how to pray against his diabolical tactics.

5 Casting down imaginations, and every high thing that exalteth itself against the knowledge of God, and bringing into captivity every thought to the obedience of Christ; (2 Corinthians 10:5)

We are admonished to pull down demonic strongholds which are deviant mindsets that resist change. Imaginations speak to negative thoughts, ideas and ideologies which hinder your progress. Spiritual Warfare Prayers require a militant stance in prayer, which is based on the authority of the Word of God. Every believer has been granted delegated power by God to bind and loose the diabolical activities of evil spirits, in the name of Jesus. When we pray Spiritual Warfare Prayers God sends His angels to help us. He expects us to use our keys of spiritual authority to gain victory over our adversary.

19 And I will give unto thee the keys of the kingdom of heaven: and whatsoever thou shalt bind on earth shall be bound in heaven: ... heaven. (Matthew 16:19a)

Persistent Prayers

Persistent Prayers are prayers you pray adamantly or tenaciously without giving up. It is praying without ceasing *(1 Thessalonians 5:17)*. It is a relentless prayer of spiritual resilience that compels you to push until you receive your desired results. Daniel demonstrated Persistent Prayer. He prayed for 21 days, gained access to the throne room of God and received angelic assistance. When you pray persistently you may also experience angelic visitation. Your Persistent Prayer will bring you into prevailing prayer and, eventually, into your victory, but you must give God no rest. Continue to come boldly before the throne of grace and "trouble" it to obtain the courage you need to overcome because your breakthrough is at hand *(Hebrews 4:16)*.

Prayers of Prosperity

¹⁹ And he called the name of that place Bethel: but the name of that city was called Luz at the first.

²⁰ And Jacob vowed a vow, saying, If God will be with me, and will keep me in this way that I go, and will give me bread to eat, and raiment to put on,

²¹ So that I come again to my father's house in peace; then shall the LORD be my God:

²² And this stone, which I have set for a pillar, shall be God's house: and of all that thou shalt give me I will surely give the tenth unto thee. (Genesis 28:19 – 22)

Prosperity means God has abundantly blessed you to the degree that you are in a thriving, flourishing state. You live in the realm of abundance and have a good, healthy disposition spiritually, physically, mentally, emotionally and financially. It means that you are complete, content and fully satisfied in your *body, soul and spirit.*

Although prosperity often includes wealth, it does not mean that if you have a lot of money you are fulfilled or automatically prosperous. Rather it speaks to the fact that you have been liberated by the Spirit of God to a realm of total freedom where nothing stresses you out.

Health, strength, peace, love, joy and happiness are all a part of a God-filled life. Wealth is also a part of prosperity. However, there are many wealthy people who are very unhappy and tormented in their minds.

Therefore, having wealth alone does not dictate a prosperous life. I believe that one of the greatest secrets to becoming prosperous according to God's standards and receiving answers to Prayers of Prosperity is to make a vow to God to bless His kingdom.

> *17 He that hath pity upon the poor lendeth unto the LORD; and that which he hath given will he pay him again. (Proverbs 19:17)*

The Spirit of God has already revealed that it is the will of the Father that we should prosper and be in health, even as our souls prosper.

> *Beloved, I wish above all things that thou mayest prosper and be in health, even as thy soul prospereth (3 John 1:2)*

As you earnestly pray the Prayer of Prosperity you will soon discover that there is nothing lacking and nothing broken in your life. You will begin to feel entirely whole in body, soul and spirit.

I declare and prophesy that the blessings of Almighty God will be upon your mind, in your health, your finances, your family and in every area that concerns you. I also declare, more than all, that your soul will prosper in Jesus name.

Prayers of Forgiveness

The power of forgiveness is a prerequisite to any area of healing, deliverance or progress in your life. Prayers of Forgiveness release you from the anger, bitterness, and resentment you feel toward someone who has done you wrong or grossly offended you. You fully release them and no longer blame them or require retribution from them. The Prayer of Forgiveness releases you from this personal struggle and brings about inner healing. It does not mean that you forget what has happened to you, but it does mean that you relinquish the yoke of unforgiveness, setting our soul free. Failing to forgive will hinder your prayers and eventually destroy your life.

> *25 And when ye stand praying, forgive, if ye have ought against any: that your Father also which is in heaven may forgive you your trespasses.*
> *(Mark 11:25)*

Prayers of Healing

It is not the will of God that we should live in bondage to any type of sickness or disease. Sickness is a curse from the enemy and is controlled by the strongman called *infirmity*. Under the influence of the strongman of infirmity are all manner of diseases and disorders. It is not God's will that you live under such bondage.

The ultimate goal of the spirit of infirmity is to cause death. God's will is for you is to live an abundant life free from pain and sickness. ***James 5:15 states that the prayer of faith heals the sick.***

God is Jehovah Rapha, the God who heals, and healing is available for you. Therefore, if you are believing for healing for yourself or a loved one you must aggressively pray the Prayer of Healing, in faith.

Start by acknowledging that God is your Healer through the blood of Jesus Christ. Command the sickness, by its name, to go from your body now in Jesus' name. Utilize the *12 Minutes to Breakthrough Prayer Strategy* to gain victory and total healing. Adamantly declare victory over whatever is seeking to bring affliction to your life, in Jesus' name!

Prayers of Deliverance

[13] And lead us not into temptation, but deliver us from evil: For thine is the kingdom, and the power, and the glory, for ever. Amen. (Matthew 6:13)

The Prayer of Deliverance is needed when there is a desperate desire to be set free from bondage or a stronghold of the enemy. It is a strategic prayer aimed at bringing you or someone from a place of oppression to a life of total victory.

Deliverance is a decision. In other words, you must choose to be free. Pray this type of prayer by first acknowledging the spirit that is binding you; be willing to sever ties with every demonic spirit then bind them and cast them out, commanding them to leave your life in Jesus' name.

[36] If the Son therefore shall make you free, ye shall be free indeed. (John 8:36)

Prayers of Breakthrough

Jesus is the Lord of the Breakthrough! The Prayer of Breakthrough should only be prayed when you are truly desperate, in dire need of a breakthrough and understand that He is the only way out of your situation.

Breakthrough prayers are radical, **strong-willed** prayers which do not accept "No" for an answer. When you pray such prayers it means that you will not stop until you possess total victory.

By definition, **breakthrough** means the removal of a barrier to facilitate progress or the act of penetrating the enemy's line and returning with the victory.

As a believer you can gain your breakthrough in prayer by engaging your spiritual weapons of warfare, which includes praise, declaring the Word of God and pleading the blood of Jesus.

Prayers of Travail or Lamentation

In the Word of God there are several accounts of prayers of travail or lamentation. This is the type of prayer that moves God; one where your soul is poured out to Him. People who pray in this manner have laid aside pride, self-consciousness, the opinions of others and haughtiness.

One example of this in scripture is the account of Hannah in **1 Samuel 1**. She went to the altar at the temple and earnestly prayed before God. This prayer of travail and lamentation causes you to become so broken that you can hardly utter words.

In the presence of God, Hannah released all of her pent up anguish and bitterness. She was so demonstrative during her prayer that she appeared to be drunk **(1 Samuel 1:12-18)**. Eli, the priest, did not recognize this type of intoxicating, consuming, passionate prayer, for he thought that she was under the influence of wine or strong drink.

When a woman is about to give birth she is said to be in travail; there is a cry that resonates from within her. Likewise, when you are about to give birth to something spiritually you may also engage in some level of travailing prayer. You find yourself crying out to God from the depths of your soul until He hears you.

> *⁶ This poor man cried, and the LORD heard him,*
> *and saved him out of all his troubles.*
> *(Psalm 34:6)*

There is an innumerable number of prayers that can be prayed. Your petition and request to God is determined by what you are facing at the time. I will define some of the many other types of prayers you can pray in my upcoming book on prayer.

THE NAMES OF GOD

Over the years I have discovered that I received greater victories as I added more spiritual attributes to my prayer. There were times that I used some of the names of God, and especially the Word of God, during my times of prayer and worship. This added greater dimensions to my prayer and helped me to achieve desired results. You can also use the names of God and the Word of God in your prayers and watch Him move mightily on your behalf.

In **Exodus 3** Moses asked God His name and God told him that His name was, "I Am!" As you begin to call

Him by His name, He causes whatever you ask of Him to manifest. If you see Him as your Deliverer, then He will deliver you. If you see him as your Healer, then He will heal you. If you see Him as your Redeemer, then He will redeem you. Whatever you see Him as is what He will become to you. He is the Sovereign God and He does not change; He is faithful.

I encourage you to pray the names of God, as you engage your **12 Days of Breakthrough Prayer at 12 Noon and 12 Midnight for 12 Minutes**. This not only reminds you of the manifested nature of God, it also lets God know that you esteem and honor Him for who He is, the Ultimate Source of every victory in your life. Pray using the names of God during your midnight seasons, and watch your breakthrough unfold as God, Himself answers **your Midnight Cry.**

Here are some of the names of God and their meaning:
- **EL ELOAH:** *God; **El** means mighty or strong God; "mighty, strong, powerful, prominent" (Psalm 18:31; Psalm 139:19)*

- **ELOHIM:** *God "Creator, Mighty and Strong" (Genesis 1:1, Genesis 17:7; Jeremiah 31:33)*

- **EL SHADDAI:** *"God Almighty," "The Mighty One of Jacob" (Genesis 17:1, Genesis 49:24; Psalm 132:2, 5)*

- **ADONAI:** *"Lord" (Genesis 15:2; Judges 6:15) – used in place of JEHOVAH (which is esteemed in* *the Jewish culture as the most reverend and sacred name for God)*

- **JEHOVAH:** *"LORD GOD" (Deuteronomy 6:4; Daniel 9:14) This name of God was first revealed to Moses through the burning bush as "I Am who I Am" (Exodus 3:14)*

- **JEHOVAH-JIREH:** *"The Lord Will Provide" (Genesis 22:14) – the name memorialized by Abraham when God provided the ram to be sacrificed in place of his son, Isaac.*

- **JEHOVAH-RAPHA:** *"The Lord My Healer" (Exodus 15:26)*

- **JEHOVAH-NISSI:** *"The Lord Our Banner or Sign of Victory" (Exodus 17:15; Exodus 17)*

- **JEHOVAH-MEKADDISHKEM (M'KADDESH):** *"The Lord my Sanctifier, The Lord Who Makes Me Holy" (Exodus31:13; Leviticus 20:8; Ezekiel 20:12; Ezekiel 37:28)*

- **JEHOVAH-SHALOM:** *"The Lord My Peace" (Judges 6:24)*

- **JEHOVAH-ELOHIM:** *"The Eternal Creator or the Self-Existent One" (Genesis 2:4-25)*

- **JEHOVAH-ELYOWN:** *"The Lord Most High" (Psalm 7:17; Psalm 47:2; Psalm 97:9)*

- **JEHOVAH-HOSEENU:** *"The Lord our Maker"* *(Psalm 95:6)*

- **JEHOVAH-ELOHEENU:** *"The Lord Our God"* *(Psalm 99:5, 8, 9)*

- **JEHOVAH-ELOHEKA:** *"The Lord My God"* *(Exodus 20:2, 5, 7)*

- **JEHOVAH-ELOHAY:** *"The Lord My God"* *(Zechariah 14:5)*

- **JEHOVAH-TSIDKENU:** *"The Lord Our Righteousness" (Jeremiah 23:6 ; Jeremiah 33:16 2 Corinthians 5:21)*

- **JEHOVAH-ROHI:** *"The Lord My Shepherd" (Psalm 23:1)*

- **JEHOVAH-SHAMMAH:** *"The Lord Who Is There (For Me); The Lord Is Present" (Ezekiel 48:35)*

- **JEHOVAH-SABBAOTH:** *"The Lord of Hosts" (Isaiah 1:24; Psalm 46:7; 1 Samuel 1:3)*

- **EL ELYON:** *"The Most High God" (Genesis 14:18-20; Psalm 57:2)*

- **EL ROI:** *"The God who sees"(Genesis 16:1– 14)*

- **EL-OLAM:** *"Everlasting God" (Genesis 21:33; Psalm 90:1-3)*

- **EL-GIBHOR:** *"The Mighty God; Warrior" (Isaiah 9:6; Revelation 19:15)*

****

*"What Are The Different Names Of God And What Do They Mean?" got Questions.com **Got Questions Ministries.** © 2002–2016

CHAPTER SEVEN

THE MIDNIGHT CRY

THE MIDNIGHT CRY

There are two aspects of midnight. There is the midnight of actual time and there is the midnight that represents a symbolic season of time.

Chronologically, midnight may be considered as one of the darkest hours of the day. Midnight can also symbolically represent the dark seasons, dilemmas, demonic attacks, trials and other challenges you may face. At some point in your life you will go through what I call a **midnight battle**. This is a very harsh season of demonic warfare that is governed by a fierce demon called **the spirit of darkness**.

The demon of darkness attacks and manifests in a number of ways, namely as:
- *the dark places*
- *the hard places*
- *the places of spiritual warfare*
- *the seasons of dilemmas and hardships*

❖ **The Midnight of the Dark Places** represents encounters so horrific and devastating that they cause *darkness* and sorrow to your soul. Everything appears hopeless and it becomes difficult for you to see your way out of your problems. It is during the seasons of darkness when there seems to be no light or spiritual insight that you may lose your sense of direction and may even lose your focus.

This experience is coupled with immense heaviness, discouragement and despair. At times it may come upon you like a blanket; no matter how hard you try, it is difficult to remove. It may feel like the *weight of death* as you become overburdened and weighed down.

During the midnight of the dark places many demonic spirits will try to attack you, but the ruling spirit that will lead the attack is the strongman of heaviness. This is a master demonic spirit that slowly wears out its victims. It works with the python spirit to slowly suffocate you, luring you into the dark places by using spirits of hurt and pain along with a battalion of demonic collaborations.

Some of the other cohorts or affiliating demons which seek to attach themselves to you during the Midnight Season of the Dark Places are:

- the spirit of Depression
- the spirit of Loneliness
- the spirit of Murder
- the spirit of Self-pity
- the spirit of Isolation
- the spirit of Hopelessness
- the spirit of Low Self-Esteem
- the spirit of Despair
- the spirit of *Not Good Enough*
- the spirit of Suicide
- the spirit of Discouragement
- the spirit of Death
- and many others

❖ **The Midnight of Hard Places** represents problems or situations which are vexing to the soul. These are the seasons when most people ask God, "Why?" and tend to walk away from things that matter. The Midnight of Hard Places finds you at crossroads, having to make life-altering decisions even when you do not know what to do. During the midnight of hard places most people find themselves under the attack of demon spirits of limitation and suppression.

Some other cohorts or affiliating demons which seek to attach themselves to you during the Midnight Season of Hard Places are:

- the spirit of Frustration
- the spirit of Immobility
- the spirit of Stagnation
- the spirit of Hindrance
- the spirit of Instability
- the spirit of Insecurity
- the spirit of Self-pity
- the spirit of Doubt
- the spirit of Unbelief
- the spirit of Restriction
- the spirit of Indecision
- the spirit of Confusion
- the spirit of Fear
- the spirit of The *"What if?"* Syndrome'
- and more

God promises in His Word that He will never leave or forsake you. Rather, He goes before your difficulties and trials to break through the hard places on your behalf.

> *² I will go before thee, and make the crooked places straight: I will break in pieces the gates of brass, and cut in sunder the bars of iron:*
> *(Isaiah 45:2)*

❖ *The Midnight Places of Spiritual Warfare* represents relentless, diabolical attacks which are orchestrated by the enemy to bring destruction and devastation to your life. It is satan's ultimate intention for you to concede to what you are going through. During this season you are wrestling with all manner of demonic spirits, including spirits of *fear, torment, pride and doubt.*

Some other cohorts or affiliating demons which seek to attach themselves to you during *the Midnight of Spiritual Warfare* **season are:**

- the spirit of Sleeplessness/ Insomnia
- the spirit of Mind Battles (the Embattled Mind)
- the spirit of Torment
- the spirit of Chaos
- the spirit of Lethargy
- the spirit of Anguish
- the spirit of Hurt
- the spirit of Pain
- the spirit of Destruction
- the spirit of Anger
- the spirit of Rage
- the spirit of Resentment
- the spirit of Defeat
- the spirit of Failure
- the spirit of Disappointment
- the spirit of Distress
- the spirit of Regret
- the spirit of Guilt
- the spirit of Condemnation
- the spirit of Dissatisfaction
- the spirit of Displeasure
- the spirit of Fear
- the spirit of Anxiety
- the spirit of Confusion
- ...and more

❖ *The Midnight of the Seasons of Dilemmas or Hardships*

represents a season in your life when you experience perpetual adversities. This is a time in your life where one thing after another keeps going wrong. You cannot explain what is happening to you. Your life becomes a vicious cycle of bad news, hardships and struggles. This season seems never ending and, if it does come to an end, it somehow reoccurs at a later time.

> *19 For the good that I would I do not: but the evil which I would not, that I do.*
>
> *20 Now if I do that I would not, it is no more I that do it, but sin that dwelleth in me.*
>
> *21 I find then a law, that, when I would do good, evil is present with me.*
>
> *22 For I delight in the law of God after the inward man:*
>
> *23 But I see another law in my members, warring against the law of my mind, and bringing me into captivity to the law of sin which is in my members.*
>
> *24 O wretched man that I am! who shall deliver me from the body of this death?*
>
> *25 I thank God through Jesus Christ our Lord. So then with the mind I myself serve the law of*
>
> *God; but with the flesh the law of sin (Romans 7:19–25)*

GOD WORKS THE MIDNIGHT SHIFT

62At midnight I will rise to give thanks unto thee because of thy righteous judgments.
(Psalms 119:62)

There may be times in your life when it appears that your prayers have taken a detour from the throne room and gone somewhere else. In these midnight occurrences you may think that God has forgotten you and is not concerned about your vexing problem. He has not!

You may be asking, "What is God doing while I am in a desperate need of a breakthrough?" The answer is, God has not forgotten you, He is working the *midnight shift* to bring about supernatural miracles on your behalf!

6 And when Herod would have brought him forth, the same night Peter was sleeping between two soldiers, bound with two chains: and the keepers before the door kept the prison.

7 And, behold, the angel of the Lord came upon him, and a light shined in the prison: and he smote Peter on the side, and raised him up, saying, Arise up quickly. And his chains fell off from his hands. (Acts 12:6–7)

Herod arrested and imprisoned Peter with the intent to have him executed. He assigned 16 soldiers to guard Peter and chained him between two additional soldiers but God sent an angel to deliver him. When you are in your midnight season and the enemy is celebrating your imminent death, if you cry out to God He hears you and, ultimately, rescues you.

⁶ This poor man cried, and the LORD heard him, and saved him out of all his troubles. (Psalm 34:6)

HOW THE ENEMY ABUSES YOUR MIDNIGHT

Abuse is the abnormal or incorrect use of something. The enemy is so evil and cunning that he seeks to turn around for evil everything Father God gives us for blessings. It is the will of God that every season in your life brings peace, joy and contentment. However, the enemy attempts to take advantage of your dark seasons by causing much pain and grief.

Another parable put he forth unto them, saying, The kingdom of heaven is likened unto a man which sowed good seed in his field:

But while men slept, his enemy came and sowed tares among the wheat, and went his way.

But when the blade was sprung up, and brought forth fruit, then appeared the tares also. (Matthew 13:24–26)

The parable explains what happens when you, as a believer, are spiritually asleep or spiritually unconscious; meaning you are totally unaware of what is happening around you. It also serves to represent moments of spiritual weakness or times of inopportune moments when people fall asleep and are taken advantage of by the enemy.

For example, some people, even after sleeping all night, still spend most of their day sleeping. Others may find that even during the day, they suddenly fall asleep anywhere. I call this **spiritual narcolepsy.**

Narcolepsy is a neurological disorder that is characterized by an extreme tendency of falling asleep anywhere, especially during the day. Although this can be medically diagnosed, I believe that this is really the attack of the enemy. This is a demon spirit that releases the spirit of heaviness.

Narcolepsy comes from the Greek word **Narke'** which means numbness and its English **Epilepsy.** People who suffer from either of these disabilities generally experience *sleep paralysis* which causes them to fall into a deep sleep during prayer, reading the Bible or listening to a message preached from the Word of God.

The New Age Movement and Scientology have tried to disguise or scientifically explain the activity of the demonic realm with various theories and hypotheses. For example, they use the word **hypnopomic** to describe what we call "hagging", which occurs when you feel another presence that is invisible in a room or like you are falling off of a building or being pressed on a bed. These are demons which have illegally invaded your life.

For this reason many people who work in prophetic or deliverance ministries are sometimes attacked and, at times, can feel dysfunctional, especially those who are a part of **Media and Publications**. The same may happen to people who work in other areas in full-time ministry. They regularly feel fatigued and tired.

The demonic spirits associated with demonic narcolepsy are:

- Chronic Fatigue
- Sleep Paralysis
- Epilepsy
- Seizure
- Migraines
- Forgetfulness
- Confusion
- Fear
- Torment
- Delusions
- Hypnosis
- Hallucination/ (Between Sleep and Wake)
- Dysfunction
- Impotence
- Frigidity
- Insanity
- Arrested Development
- Sleep Walking
- Sleep Talking

The demon of narcolepsy is a demon that literally sits on the head or shoulders of a person until they become extremely drowsy and fall asleep. Once the person falls asleep and lays down it sits on his back causing the person to feel paralyzed. *All of these conditions are associated with demonic attacks. You must earnestly seek God for total deliverance.*

DEFEATING THE SPIRIT OF SLUMBER

The enemy constantly attacks the believer using various methods. He subtly tries to lull you to sleep, causing you to enter a season of ***spiritual slumber***. During this season of spiritual slumber your soul can become dry because you are overwhelmed by the cares of life and unaware of what he is doing. Prolonged spiritual slumber can lead to a life of misery and frustration.

While you are physically asleep your enemy, the devil, is undoubtedly awake and often uses this time to sow his demonic seeds into your mind. One of the enemy's greatest deceptions is sowing *tares* or setbacks among the blessings God has given you. He disguises himself in sheep's clothing and creeps into your life to bring devastation and total destruction.

> *15 Beware of false prophets, which come to you in sheep's clothing, but inwardly they are ravening wolves. (Matthew 7:15)*

It is therefore incumbent upon every believer to remain prayerful and vigilant in order to counter the diabolical strategies of the enemy, including those people who deceptively pretend to be godly but are actually wolves in sheep's clothing.

> *Be sober, be vigilant; because your adversary the devil, as a roaring lion, walketh about, seeking whom he may devour: (1 Peter 5:8)*

There are dark seasons which I call *midnight*. There is also the actual time of night that is called midnight that some people call **The Bewitching Hour**. The devil specifically launches his attacks at midnight. It is generally during the hours between *midnight and 3:00 a.m.* that the wicked seek to carry out many of their evil plans against the righteous; unfortunately, with little to no resistance from believers.

This is unfortunate, however, because it is during this time when intercessors and prayer warriors are able to gain their greatest victories over the power and influence of witches.   I call this **the Holy Ghost Hour of Power!**

For the most part many Christians are in deep sleep during this time.   When you are asleep the devil sends his demons of terror to alter and manipulate the events of your next day before you awake.   He sends fear and torment along with other demons which are on assignment to create a snare for you as you enter your day.

MIDNIGHT MADNESS

²And it was told the Gazites, saying, Samson is come hither. And they compassed him in, and laid wait for him all night in the gate of the city, and were quiet all the night, saying, In the morning, when it is day, we shall kill him. (Judges 16:2)

There are some midnights of hardships which you face because you may not have followed God's instructions.   Nevertheless, if you earnestly pray He is merciful to forgive you and make a way of escape.

In **Judges 16** Samson was faced with a life or death situation that propelled him into a midnight experience.   He found himself in a dilemma because he entered the enemy's territory to satisfy his own fleshly desires. He wanted Delilah and was prepared to do whatever it took to have her.

When Samson's enemies, the Philistines, realized that he was on their territory, they plotted to capture him and then kill him. This, no doubt, became the darkest hour in the life of Samson.

Samson's turning point came when he arose at midnight to engage his battle strategy against his enemies. The Bible says that *Samson waited until midnight when they went to sleep before he planned his escape.* **This time he would not confront his enemies but would escape out of their hands.**

³ And Samson lay till midnight, and arose at midnight, and took the doors of the gate of the city, and the two posts, and went away with them, bar and all, and put them upon his shoulders, and carried them up to the top of an hill that is before Hebron. (Judges 16:3)

Had Samson fallen asleep during the midnight hour his enemies would have killed him. Instead, Samson remained awake, waited until his enemies went to sleep and then he acted. As a warrior you must remain vigilant and not fall asleep in the time of warfare. You must fight through your midnight seasons trusting God for divine intervention over demonic confederations.

DEMONIC COURT SESSIONS

Throughout the night, the enemy seeks to conduct demonic court sessions in the invisible spirit realm which are designed to bring railing accusations against you. He hires false demonic witnesses to negatively represent you and defame your character. This happens mostly when you are asleep or during your seasons of hardship.

Evil lords and judges from these demonic courts pass judgment on you and falsely sentence you, unjustly releasing upon you curses of sickness, disease, failure, financial hardship and more.

By the time you awake the following morning you feel burdened with a spirit of guilt, shame and condemnation. You may even feel perplexed and overwhelmed beyond what you are able to explain. Paul charged the believers in the church at Ephesus to awake from their sleep or state of spiritual unconsciousness to a new realm of spiritual illumination.

> *14 **Wherefore he saith, Awake thou that sleepest, and arise from the dead, and Christ shall give thee light (Ephesians 5:14)***

Everyone deserves rest and sound sleep but when that time of rest is over, God is calling you to be spiritually awake and conscious. As kingdom warriors, believers should be spiritually sound and armed to combat the infiltrations of the enemy, even those which come through the night watches.

In the natural realm you must be prepared to spend time during the day and night watches, building yourself up spiritually. You must condition yourself to rest while remaining alert and focused on God's divine plan. Never sleep so deeply that you are not aware of your surroundings.

DESTINY SLAYERS OF THE NIGHT

As a child of God, your divine destiny is the ultimate plan of blessings which Almighty God has for you. Satan does not ever want you to come into that plan, therefore he uses your night seasons against you in order to sabotage God's will and purpose for your life.

It is during these seasons when you must have confidence in the Word of God concerning you.

3 Surely he shall deliver thee from the snare of the fowler, and from the noisome pestilence.

4 He shall cover thee with his feathers, and under his wings shalt thou trust: his truth shall be thy shield and buckler.

5 Thou shalt not be afraid for the terror by night; nor for the arrow that flieth by day;

6 Nor for the pestilence that walketh in darkness; nor for the destruction that wasteth at noonday. (Psalm 91:3–6)

The Spirit of God taught me how to fight at almost every level. He showed me how the enemy uses an army of evil spirits to sabotage people's destinies during nights of dark seasons if nothing is done to counter their attack.

In **Psalm 91** there are four squadrons of demons revealed: *The Terror by Night, The Arrow That Flieth by Day, The Pestilence That Walketh in Darkness* and *The Destruction That Wasteth at Noonday.*

The Terror By Night – Terror by night refers to evil spirits which work with the strongman of the spirit of fear and torment. This spirit is a ruler of the darkness usually exercising his power during the night and even to a greater degree during dark seasons of your life. It produces a deeper darkness to the soul causing stress, anxiety, sleeplessness, depression and suicidal thoughts.

The Destruction That Wasteth At Noonday
– These are evil spirits which work with the demons called
Arrows. In Revelation 9:11 the demon of destruction is
called *Abbadon*. His Greek name is *Apollyon (the
destroyer); their counterpart co-conspirator is called
Asmodeus, the destroying one.*

Their diabolical assignment is not just to wear you
down but to wear you out, ultimately destroying you.
They work best at noonday, in the middle of your
moments of decision. Destruction is a master principality
ruling a battalion of demonic assassins whose deathly
assignment is to kill, steal and destroy *(John 10:10).* He
seeks to shut down any possibility of spiritual, physical
and financial progress in your life by using the spirits of
limitation, hindrance and sabotage to stop you.

The Arrow That Flieth By Day – These evil
spirits work through piercing negative thoughts which
attack your mind. They can operate through oppressive
and slanderous words spoken to afflict and wound your
soul. Further, **The Arrows** can also work through verbal
or emotional abuse. Their vice grip on your mind can
painstakingly destroy you if you allow it to dominate your
thoughts. You become overwhelmed by negative or ill-
spoken words. You even become afflicted in your body
because of stress and worry. These demonic arrows shoot,
not only at your mind, but may also be shot at your back
through spell crafts and curses to break your back, hence,
your strength, causing you to become spiritually paralyzed
and weak.

**The Pestilence That Walketh In Darkness
and the Terror of the Night** are strongman
principalities which work together to dispatch other

demonic spirits against your life to produce tragedy and torture during your dark seasons. They create problems of massive proportions like plagues or persistent, heart-wrenching circumstances that do not want to go away. They are stubborn demons that will wait until you are at a weak, vulnerable point before they seek to take advantage of you.

No matter which area of ministry you have been called to, you will experience some level of this type of warfare. As you bombard heaven and observe the various watches of the day and night with consistent prayer you will become more and more victorious. God will send His angels to deliver you from such evil spirits.

Arriving ready to go to battle at **midnight** through spiritual warfare will position you to stop the enemy from invading your territory and setting demonic traps to sabotage your God-ordained destiny.

> *There Is A Plethora Of Weaponry And Spiritual Warfare Tactics That God Used Throughout Scripture To Give His People Victory. You Must Select Your Weapon Of Choice And Use It Skillfully.*

If the enemy can send his night slayers to try and destroy you, God can send his Rescue Agents called Angels to rescue you.

NIGHT RESCUERS

"For he shall give his angels charge over thee, to keep thee in all thy ways." (Psalm 91:11)

In **Acts 12** God sent his angels to rescue Peter from prison and did the same, in **Acts 16**, for Paul and Silas. Just as He moved supernaturally for them He will do the same for you as you call upon Him. This group of **angels** is called *Rescuers* or *Rescue Angels* and they specialize in bringing God's people out of difficult situations.

In addition to worshipping God, guarding and protecting His people from danger, is one of the things Rescuers enjoy doing most.

Just like all other angels and heavenly beings, the Rescuers move swift and travel faster than the speed of light. It was this group of angels that led the children of Israel out of Egypt rescuing them from the pursuing Pharaoh army. They took the wheels off of Pharaoh's chariots and caused chaos in their midst. These mighty angels of God are skilled in every aspect of warfare and combat.

> *²⁰And they rose early in the moring, and went into the wilderness of Tekoa: and as they went forth, Jehoshaphat stood and said, Hear me, O Judah, and ye inhabitants of Jerusalem; Believe in the LORD your God, so shall ye be established; believe his prophets, so shall ye prosper.*

> *²¹And when he had consulted with the people, he appointed singers unto the LORD, and that should praise the beauty of holiness, as they went out before the army, and to say, Praise the LORD; for his mercy endureth for ever.*

22 And when they began to sing and to praise, the LORD set ambushments against the children of Ammon, Moab, and mount Seir, which were come against Judah; and they were smitten.

23 For the children of Ammon and Moab stood up against the inhabitants of mount Seir, utterly to slay and destroy them: and when they had made an end of the inhabitants of Seir, every one helped to destroy another. (2 Chronicles 20:20–23)

In **2 Chronicles 20**, God used them to cause the armies of Moab and Seir to turn on each other. The Bible called it **ambushment.** God sent his Rescue Angels on that assignment and they released confusion in the midst of the armies of their enemies thus giving Israel the ultimate victory.

God will also rescue you. As you continue to have faith in the God of the Supernatural and never doubt, you will see miraculous rescue operations unfold before your eyes.

WINNING THE WARFARE AT MIDNIGHT

In **Ephesians 6:12** Paul admonishes us that as believers we should always be aware that our wrestling match is not against persons with physical bodies. Rather, he warns that we are in a perpetual conflict in the heavenly realm against ruling satanic spirits with various ranks and authorities. These *high ranking* evil spirits are the demonic world dominators of the present hour.

You must make every effort to defeat the realm of darkness by exposing the deceiver in your personal life and removing yourself from denial or spiritual ignorance. You can then start fighting with your spiritual artillery.

In order to win the war you must know who or what you are fighting. Every demonic spirit has a name. If you do not know their names then take careful note of their characteristics or behaviors. As you pray, you will recognize or discern their activities and Holy Spirit will teach you how to win the warfare against them.

> *3 For though we walk in the flesh, we do not war after the flesh:*

> *4 (For the weapons of our warfare [are] not carnal, but mighty through God to the pulling down of strong holds;)*
> *(2 Corinthians 10:3-4)*

With God's help you will not fail. He has already gone before you in the way to give you the victory during your times of warfare, but you must show up to the battle. You must be prepared to persevere and fight in prayer. You will not be defeated, you will win.

CALLING ALL SPIRITUAL KINGDOM WARRIORS

One of the names of God is Jehovah Gibbor which means that He is a God of war. As the Sovereign Ruler over the Kingdom of God, He is now calling you as a believer to be a spiritual kingdom warrior. A spiritual kingdom warrior is someone who has been anointed by God to wage war on behalf of the Kingdom of God.

Spiritual kingdom warriors do not quit or give up easily but, rather, they are relentless in their fight against the kingdom of darkness. A true kigndom warrior spends time in prayer, fasting, worship and reading the Word. *Some other attributes of Spiritual Kingdom Warriors are that...*

- *Spiritual Kingdom Warriors* seldom worry and know how do defeat spirits of fear, doubt and unbelief.
- *Spiritual Kingdom Warriors* are self-motivated.
- *Spiritual Kingdom Warriors* pray even when they are tired.
- *Spiritual Kingdom Warriors* keep going for God and the good of mankind!
- *Spiritual Kingdom Warriors* are not easily offended.
- *Spiritual Kingdom Warriors* are self motivated and are not moved by the negative opinions of others.
- *Spiritual Kingdom Warriors* know how to operate in seasons of famine or seasons of plenty.
- *Spiritual Kingdom Warriors* do not have time to waste.
- *Spiritual Kingdom Warriors* do not waste time playing with their enemies.
- *Spiritual Kingdom Warriors* do not succumb to the pressures of life.
- *Spiritual Kingdom Warriors* keep their eyes on the target; they are locked and fixed on their destiny.
- *Spiritual Kingdom Warriors* are resilient; they rebound quickly!
- *Spiritual Kingdom Warriors* fight to the finish!
- *Spiritual Kingdom Warriors* are always dressed and ready for battle!

CHAPTER EIGHT

ANSWERING THE CALL TO THE MIDNIGHT CRY

BLOWING THE SHOFAR

"Blow ye the trumpet in Zion, and sound an alarm in my Holy Mountain:..." (Joel 2:1)

In the prophetic realm, the trumpet is similar to the shofar because they are both symbolic of "sounding" instruments. The blowing of the trumpet signifies prophetic intercession. You are crying out to God but also warning the people of danger.

Blowing of the shofar was always a part of the Jewish culture that represents "A Midnight Cry!" The shofar was blown to announce significant events such as the New Year, the commencement of the Feast Days, the installation of a new king, the declaration of war against the enemy and others.

The spiritual significance of blowing the shofar in the life of every believer should be the same. You should be willing to open your mouth, declare the Word of God or speak truth in every situation. There should be a midnight cry in your mouth that shakes the realm of the spirit as you declare war against the enemy.

I WILL GIVE HIM NO REST

How desperate are you for your miracle? How bad do you want it? In **Luke 18** the Bible records the parable of a widow woman who demonstrated what it meant to be persistent in prayer. She had a desperate need and continually went before the one she knew could meet that need. This person was a corrupt but powerful leader, a judge. The scripture calls him **unjust.** It was her relentless determination that moved him to action, not out of compassion for her but because of her persistence.

4Though I fear not God, nor regard man;

5 Yet because this widow troubleth me, I will avenge her, lest by her continual coming she weary me.
(Luke 18:4–5)

As a result of this widow's persistence and dedication her needs were met. If determination and consistency pays off with a corrupt human of limited power, imagine how much more it will pay off with a loving, just God of unlimited, infinite power.

"I will give him no rest" must be your soul's cry if you are to see any level of breakthrough, deliverance, healing or prosperity. How desperate are you? How bad do you want your breakthrough? Are you prepared, like that widow woman, to do whatever it takes? Are you prepared to continually *make your requests known* before the Father? *(Philippians 4:6)* Are you prepared to come before God at midnight for at least *12 Minutes* to receive your breakthrough?

You must be prepared to sacrifice everything so that you can gain total victory. Abraham was willing to sacrifice his promised child so that God would be glorified *(Genesis 22:1-14)*. King David was prepared to sacrifice his dignity, as he danced before the Lord in clamorous worship and displeased his wife, Michal. He did not care how he looked in the eyes of man. All he wanted to do was please his Heavenly Father *(2 Samuel 6:9-14)*. Ruth was prepared to sacrifice her family and countrymen to be with her mother-in-law Naomi *(Ruth 1: 16-18)*. What are you prepared to sacrifice?

I will give him no rest. You must pray without ceasing according to **Luke 18:1**. *I will give him no rest.* Your prayers must be consistent. It is often said that it takes twenty-one days to either form or break a habit. ***How radically would your life change if you took the next twenty-one days and formed a habit of persistent prayer?***

THE WATCHER

A *Watcher* is considered to be a prophetic seer. God will open the eyes of His chosen watcher to see in the realm of the spirit and speak forth His divine will as the Spirit gives him utterance. Therefore the Watcher sees impending danger and, through the power of the spoken word, he can prophetically reverse it.

Although everyone in the Kingdom of God may not be prophets, I believe that God has given each one of His people a measure of grace to function in *the realm of seeing in the spirit.*

However, the depth you are willing to go in seeing in the realm of the spirit depends on you, alone. In other words, not everyone that has eyes to see beyond this natural realm follows their ability to see in the realm of the spirit.

> ***Having Spiritual Vision Is Far Greater Than Having Sight!***

For example, some people who are spiritually discerning may have inward visions or what we call strong impressions, others may have night visions or what we call dreams but few people elevate to a spiritual level of having open visions or trances.

"I have also spoken by the prophets, and I have multiplied visions, and used similitudes, by the ministry of the prophets."
(Hosea 12:10)

In the book of Genesis, when God created man in His own image He had a specific plan in mind. His plan is described in **Genesis 2:15 (AMP)**, which states, **"And the Lord God took the man and put him in the Garden of Eden to tend and guard and keep it".**

Literally, the term *to tend and to keep* is a translation of the Hebrew word **shamar,** which is primarily used for *watchmen* in Scripture. God's original intent for man was to *watch over or become a steward over* what He had created; to tend, maintain and keep it.

Further, the *terms watch, watchman, watchmen and watching* are mentioned at least 165 times in the Bible. If you were to include the terms *see* and *observe,* the subject is mentioned over 300 times, almost the same number of times as the word *prayer*.

God commands His servants to guard their posts and remain informed regarding what is happening in the land. He expects the watchman and those called to prayer to discern the spiritual climate that is in their surrounding domain.

> *[11] The burden of Dumah. He calleth to me out of Seir, Watchman, what of the night? Watchman, What of the night? (Isaiah 21:11)*

Historically, the watchman was stationed on the walls of the city so that he could observe the activity within the city and all surrounding areas.

Likewise, a watcher must be someone who is a keen discerner and is very skilled in seeing impending danger. It is the great responsibility of the watchman to warn the city of possible attacks from the enemy. The watchman is the person God anoints as a mediator: to stand in between or to stand in the gap on behalf of another person, family, church, community or nation at large.

Therefore, at any time the watchman may be called upon to give details of what is happening in the land. The watchman is expected to know and to have an answer for the spiritual climate and activity in the region in every season, especially during the times of warfare.

The whole idea of a watcher as a prophet is based on the premise that that person sees, hears, knows and speaks forth the will and counsel of God. Typically, this office can be filled by the *Prophetic Watchman, The Prophetic Watchman Intercessor* or *the Warrior Watchman.*

THE PROPHETIC WATCHMAN

"God gives you the ability to speak things which do not exist as though they did already."
(Romans 4:17)

The kingdom of darkness is equipped with its demonic battalion of spies, lookers, watchers, false prophets and demons which monitor the people of God. They monitor and record information about you to use it against you in an effort to bring your life to destruction.

On the other hand, God has a divine squadron of anointed watchmen who can also see in the realm of the spirit. He sometimes uses them to guard and protect you against the demonic probes, surveillances and radars of the enemy, one such agent is *The Prophetic Watchman.*

The Prophetic Watchman sees everything through the eyes of the Spirit of God. He not only has inward or night visions but he may also regularly experience open or multiplied visions.

The Prophet is one whom God chooses and calls as His mouthpiece. He carries a mantle for the assignment given to him and foretells, protects and brings correction to God's people as he walks in the office of the Prophet. Therefore as a prophet the Prophetic Watchman is now mandated by God to speak forth exactly what he sees.

¹Again the word of the LORD *came unto me, saying,*

² Son of man, speak to the children of thy people, and say unto them, When I bring the sword upon a land, if the people of the land take a man of their coasts, and set him for their watchman:

³ If when he seeth the sword come upon the land, he blow the trumpet, and warn the people;

⁴ Then whosoever heareth the sound of the trumpet, and taketh not warning; if the sword come, and take him away, his blood shall be upon his own head.

⁵ He heard the sound of the trumpet, and took not warning; his blood shall be upon him. But he that taketh warning shall deliver his soul.

⁶ But if the watchman see the sword come, and blow not the trumpet, and the people be not warned; if the sword come, and take any person from among them, he is taken away in his iniquity; but his blood will I require at the watchman's hand.

⁷ So thou, O son of man, I have set thee a watchman unto the house of Israel; therefore thou shalt hear the word at my mouth, and warn them from me.
(Ezekiel 33:1 – 7)

THE PROPHETIC WATCHMAN INTERCESSOR

As a Prophetic Watchman Intercessor you become the intermediary to carry the weight and problems of others, in prayer. Someone else's needs becomes interwoven in your spirit and you pray until change manifests.

As a Prophetic Watchman Intercessor you accept a position or assignment to pray for a person, family, community, nation or region. As you pray, you will develop a keen sense of discernment and become sensitive to the surrounding spiritual climate.

Additionally, as you begin to function as a Prophetic Watchman, praying and interceding, you become more aware of the will of God for the assignment that He has given you. Further, you begin to receive prophetic insight, viable solutions and answers to difficult problems.

As a Prophetic Watchman Intercessor you will find yourself crying out and travailing for God's people. You carry the spirit of prayer and can become very passionate about causes like: the sick, youth affairs, the needs of the elderly, rates of crime, political anarchy, governmental corruption, domestic violence, child abuse, human trafficking and sexual immorality.

If you find yourself passionate about such vexing issues in your family, church, community or region, it could be that God has given you a burden to pray as a Prophetic Watchman Intercessor.

6 I have set watchmen upon thy walls, O Jerusalem, which shall never hold their peace day nor night: ye that make mention of the LORD, keep not silence,

7 And give him no rest, till he establish, and till he make Jerusalem a praise in the earth.

In **Isaiah 62:6–7** the prophet proclaims that he will give God no rest until Jerusalem becomes a praise in the earth. This prophet is committed to laboring in prayer until God changes the state of his nation.

The Prophetic Watchman Intercessor is not afraid to say what he sees as he opens his mouth with humility and power. He prophesies and declares victory, even in the midst of darkness.

STANDING IN THE GAP

30 And I sought for a man among them, that should make up the hedge, and stand in the gap before me for the land, that I should not destroy it: ..." (Ezekiel 22:30)

In **Ezekiel 22:30** God reveals that He is looking for someone to stand in the gap to pray as a Prophetic Watchman in His kingdom. Intercession is the act of mediating between a problem and the solution. The Watchman is handpicked by God to stand strong, bridging the gap between dilemmas or tragedies and the time God releases the answers.

And when the people complained, it displeased the LORD: and the LORD heard it; and his anger was kindled; and the fire of the LORD burnt among them, and consumed them that were in the uttermost parts of the camp.

2 And the people cried unto Moses; and when Moses prayed unto the LORD, the fire was quenched. (Numbers 11:1–2)

Moses was a mediator who constantly interceded on behalf of the children of Israel. Whenever God wanted to punish Israel or became displeased by their actions Moses stood in the gap, reminding God of His covenants and precious promises to bless and prosper His people. As

Moses prayed for the people, God assigned others, like Aaron and Hur, to pray for him and hold up his hands.

ANOINTED TO CARRY

The Prophetic Watchman Intercessor is one who is also very passionate about the spiritual leader or Prophet whom he is serving. He helps to carry the vision of that leader in the womb of intercession. He is more dedicated to caring for the needs of the leader than his own personal needs. He is unselfish and has no personal agendas, hidden secrets or ulterior motives. He only wants to see the divine will of God accomplished without hindrances or struggle.

He also accepts the assignment of interceding and praying for the prophetic leaders' family, ministry partners and those whom they are called to reach in a community, city or region. Not many people are willing to make the kind of sacrifice that this level of intercession requires; therefore, the Spirit of God will cause you to know if you are called to this assignment.

When you accept the call as a Prophetic Watchman Intercessor, you will begin to discern the needs of your Leader and the people. As you pray, you will sense what they are going through and feel what they are experiencing. You will travail for them in your spirit until you see change. You become a carrier of their burdens and one who seeks to engage every level of spiritual warfare and prayer until their victory manifests.

Just like the Warrior Watchman, you put on spiritual military strength and transform your faith to *prophetically speak* the blessings of Almighty God. Your prayer posture may include a watchful position of pacing, walking around, kneeling or rocking back and forth.

THE WARRIOR WATCHMAN

¹⁷Now a watchman stood on the tower in Jezreel, and he saw the company of Jehu as he came, and said, "I see a company of men."
(2 Kings 9:17)

The *Warrior Watchman* is similar to the Prophetic Watchman but in addition to seeing and hearing, the warrior watchman fights aggressively in the realm of the spirit. He carries out the mandate of what the Prophetic Watchman has seen and spoken.

As a Warrior Watchman you do not haphazardly pray about the problem; you wage strategic warfare in prayer until the problem is resolved or eradicated. You use prophetic gestures such as hand and foot movements, like a fighting warrior would.

They shall run like mighty men; they shall climb the wall like men of war; and they shall march every one on his ways, and they shall not break their ranks: (Joel 2:7)

As your name suggests, you are a warrior in the spirit and will not stop praying and fasting until there is total breakthrough. You are a power intercessor who boldly prays for every situation as the Spirit of God gives you revelation. You are not afraid to wage war at any level and will not stop until the battle is won.

As the Warrior Watchman, you never throw in the towel; you are prepared to stay on your watch regardless of what is happening around you and you fight to the place of victory.

> *² I will stand upon my watch, and set me upon the tower, and will watch to see what he will say unto me, and what I shall answer when I am reproved. (Habakkuk 2:1)*

THE PROPHETIC GATEKEEPER

"Agents of the Spiritual Armed Forces"

As the name suggests, the Gatekeeper is a person who stands at a gate, door or other point of entry, like a doorman, to oversee who or what comes in or goes out of the place he is assigned to monitor.

In the spiritual aspect Prophetic Gatekeepers have the same function. God anoints them with a specific mandate to stand guard at an entrance or doorway in the realm of the spirit to monitor, protect or influence the spiritual climate in a region. It is at these points of entry that people can either be defeated or victorious.

> *For a day in thy courts is better than a thousand. I had rather be a doorkeeper in the house of my God, than to dwell in the tents of wickedness. (Psalm 84:10)*

A Prophetic Gatekeper is the person appointed by God with a specific assignment to guard and protect the interests of the Kingdom of God in a famiy, region or nation.

Many blessings have been stolen by the enemy while on its way to you or your loved ones. Prophetic Gatekeepers are anointed to ensure the safe arrival of every miracle and breakthrough given to you by God.

In essence, both the gatekeeper and the watchman are, by far, considered to be very valuable spiritual officers in the kingdom. This is because they are responsible for ensuring the safety and well-being of the ministry, the citizens, their leaders and the kingdom on the whole.

As a Prophetic Gatekeeper you can only accomplish this task with the guidance and empowerment of Holy Spirit. He releases His angels to work *with* you and *for* you to help you receive supernatural help to push through your dark and challenging seasons. Further, as a Prophetic Gatekeeper you have the power to bind and loose every demonic trespasser, handcuffing them in the realm of the spirit.

> [18] *Verily I say unto you, Whatsoever ye shall bind on earth shall be bound in heaven: and whatsoever ye shall loose on earth shall be loosed in heaven.*
> *(Matthew 18:18)*

Their function as a spiritual agent is similar to that of the men and women of the armed forces who are commissioned to protect the national borders. Gatekeepers and watchmen are responsible for watching, protecting, guarding or keeping the kingdom through prayer and intercession. ***They are Spiritual National Security (SNS).***

Whenever these gatekeepers are absent, you and even the church at large can become vulnerable to the attacks of the enemy from all points.

God's Prophetic Watchman Intercessors and Gatekeepers must be ready to fight at all times and at all levels. There are three basic levels or assignments in which these watchmen intercessors are called to function:

1. **THE FIRST LEVEL – A Personal Level:** At a personal level you accept the responsibility to watch over the well-being of your soul and that of your family; you identify erroneous beliefs or practices and differentiate them from truth. You evaluate what you believe and accept as standards, morals or principles for your family to adopt in alignment with the Word of God.

He that hath no rule over his own spirit is like a city that is broken down, and without walls.
(Proverbs 25:28)

> *Wage War Against Every Demonic Attack Against Your Life And Family.*

2. **THE SECOND LEVEL – A Church Level:** interceding on behalf of the ministry and the overall well-being of the church; you are the quality control agent or spiritual filter who can help your leaders to clear the church of spiritual contaminants and help prevent spiritual poisons from infiltrating the Body of Christ.

> *¹⁰ For a day in thy courts is better than a thousand.*
> *I had rather be a doorkeeper in the house of my*
> *God, than to dwell in the tents of wickedness.*
> *(Psalm 84:10)*

3. **THE THIRD LEVEL – A National Level:** You are responsible for guarding and monitoring the moral and social standards in your society, some of which include: laws which are passed, the spiritual climate, the culture, and the overall spiritual development of the nation. You pray that curses are broken from over your nation and that your government, in addition to enforcing its national laws and bi-laws, would simultaneously, uphold biblical laws and perpetuate biblical practices.

Whenever the enemy challenges or bombards any of these areas it is your duty, as both the spiritual gatekeeper and watchman, to stand and wage war against every demonic intrusion. ***For this reason, answering the clarion call to the midnight cry is essential.***

> *"...except the* LORD *keep the city, the*
> *watchman waketh but in vain."*
> *(Psalm 127:1b)*

God is calling you to the midnight cry and He wants you to stand as a guard in the realm of the spirit. Failing to recognize your position in God as a gatekeeper or watcher can result in the total destruction of your family, local church and city. However, embracing the fact that you are called by God to stand watch and be a true keeper enables the Kingdom of God to move with great power while gaining victory at every level.

SHARPSHOOTERS:
"Waging Strategic Warfare!"

From the very first day that you got saved you were automatically enlisted in a spiritual war. This war takes place in the invisible realm and rages on between the Kingdom of God and the kingdom of satan. However, the Kingdom of God is guaranteed to emerge victorious during every battle. As a believer you are called to fight the good fight of faith, by employing spiritual weapons, such as prayer and interession, on behalf of the winning team *(1 Timothy 6:12)*.

A natural army has many ranks and positions. The army of God also has various **prayer ranks and positions** such as: intercessors, prayer warriors, seers, watchers, sharpshooters and more.

A marksman, or **sharpshooter**, *is a person who is skilled in precision shooting, using projectile weapons, such as a specialty application rifle for shooting long range targets.*

As it is in the natural, so it is in the spiritual. A spiritual sharpshooter is a prayer agent who has been mandated by the Spirit of God to strategically pray with precision, waging war against the kingdom of darkness in order to gain total victory over the enemy. These prophetic warriors are well equipped with the Word of God and are extremely dangerous to satan's kingdom.

They strategically aim at and hit every target of the enemy, annihilating his diabolical plans.

> *"...the effectual fervent prayer of a righteous man availeth much." (James 5:16b)*

To advance as a sharp shooter in the realm of the spirit you must begin by praying effective, fervent and militant prayers. ***For your prayers to produce the desired results you must consider the following:***

- You must see your target or goal and identify the specific needs which warrant prayer.

- Use the spirit of discernment to help you decide on a prayer strategy and to determine which type of prayer you should pray.

- Take your aim in the realm of the spirit, declaring God's Word, speaking specifically to the fulfillment of that need. Also, declare destruction to the enemy's stronghold.

- You must continuously give God thanks, glory and honor for the victory until it manifests in the physical realm. Delay is not denial.

Although you may continue to wage an intense warfare against the enemy in prayer, at times your problem may persist. In such instances, your prayer can intensify so as to enlist the assistance of others and become like a *battering ram*.

PRAYER AS A BATTERING RAM

In medieval times kings were concerned about expanding their kingdoms, dominating territories and acquiring new lands. Cities were built, established and fortified by massive walls and great iron gates. These were erected in order to protect the city and its interests, but also to keep their enemies out. There were guards posted at the gates and no one entered or exited without the approval of the appointed gatekeeper.

Therefore, whenever one kingdom sought to overthrow, dominate or take control of another, a fierce war ensued. Many primitive weapons, such as swords, spears, bows and arrows were used to engage in one-to-one combat with each side seeking to claim the ultimate victory in the fight. As the battle intensified and the aggressor sought to *take the entire city*, a greater military weapon called a **battering ram** was used in to order to break through the barrier of the huge city gates.

In some instances the battering ram was built to look similar to a massive ram's head mounted on the end of a long tree trunk or beam. The structure was so massive that it required a battalion of strong men to transport it to the gate of the city.

As the battle continued with flaming arrows shooting everywhere, swords clanging and some soldiers succumbing to the ravages of war, a battalion of strong men would each take a position at set points on the beam.

At the Commanding Officer's instruction, in synchronized fashion, they would back away from then charge towards the gigantic gate and, with full force, run towards it and "ram" the head of this massive weapon into it. This action was repeated until they had broken through the gate and gained entry into the city.

Once those brave warriors had gone ahead of the battle and broken through the gates of the city the entire army would lay siege to it and stake claim to this new territory. They would then seize the city, imprison the armed men and establish their own governing laws and regulations.

In this hour the Spirit of God is seeking to release a *battering ram anointing* upon the lives of His people in order to take over domains, territories and regions.

This prayer strategy requires a unified effort amongst prayer warriors, intercessors and the like. ***There are some adversaries you face which are difficult to defeat in your strength alone and you must enlist the assistance of fellow spiritual comrades.***

- God is calling His people to use their **faith** as *a battering ram*; to persist in prayer until they break through into new realms and dimensions in the spirit realm.

- God is calling His people to use their **tongue** as *a battering ram*; to persist in prophetic declarations and decrees until every godly prophetic word manifests in their lives.

- God is calling His people to use their **giving** as *a battering ram*; to persist in sowing seeds into the kingdom until their harvest is realized.

- God is calling His people to use **prophetic intercession** as *a battering ram*; to persist in corporate intercession until a change takes place in their communities, regions, countries and nations

The *battering ram anointing* in prayer requires unity in the spirit and will gain great results if used in wisdom. On many occasions I have had to mobilize my Ministry Team to employ this prayer strategy especially when traveling on mission trips to areas we called *stronghold territories.*

These territories were typically under great spiritual oppression and controlled by ruling demonic principalities. For example, as we went into areas where there were high levels of prostitution, drug and alcohol abuse, witchcraft activity and more, we saw these areas as spiritual battlegrounds.

Before entering the battlefield, we knew that we would have to bombard the realm of the spirit in order to gain the victory. *We literally came together like a battalion of soldiers to wage warfare through prayer in our effort to gain new territories for the Kingdom of God.* We unified our efforts of relentlessly bombarding the realm of the spirit, through powerful intercession, during the various prayer watches on a 24-hour period until the assignment was over or the battle was won.

The force of our combined corporate prayer acted like a battering ram in the realm of the spirit, subduing demonic resistances and dethroning mighty, ungodly giants. Once our team of intercessors were able to break through satanic forces which were set up over that region to resist the move of God, many souls were saved, delivered and set free as the strongholds of the enemy were destroyed through prayer.

CHAPTER NINE

WATCH AND PRAY

WATCH AND PRAY

40 And he cometh unto the disciples, and findeth them asleep, and saith unto Peter, What, could ye not watch with me one hour?
(Matthew 26:40)

God is calling believers to remain watchful and spiritually aggressive through prayer; to pray against every infiltration of the enemy; whether in their homes, churches, communities, regions or nations.

One of the greatest tragedies is for believers to experience severe casualties in spiritual warfare because they were not vigilant to stand watch against the enemy.

Many times believers suffer needless pains, disappointments or losses because they were not prepared to engage their weapons in the battle or they did nothing to counter the enemy's attack. It is, therefore incumbent upon every believer to remain spiritually alert, to watch and pray in order to resist every diabolical attack of the enemy.

36 Keep awake then and watch at all times [be discreet, attentive, and ready], praying that you may have the full strength and ability and be accounted worthy to escape all these things
(Luke 21:36)

DECLARING A "NO-FLY" ZONE

A No-Fly Zone is an area over which aircrafts are not permitted to fly. Sovereign nations or opposing military forces generally establish no-fly zones over areas they deem points of national security or highly sensitive military strongholds.

In military terms, a no-fly zone is similar to a **demilitarized zone** established by a Treatise Agreement between two contending military powers. Within such a zone no type of military personnel, activity or stronghold is permitted. In the United States of America the air space over the White House is a no-fly zone. If any type of aircraft is detected within a certain radius of the White House the U.S. Armed Forces both have the right and military skill to attack that aircraft, no questions asked.

In the book of Exodus God activated a *spiritual no-fly zone* over the children of Israel while they were in bondage in Egypt. The no-fly zone was established because, in obedience to God, the children of Israel applied the blood of lambs on the windows and door posts of their homes. Therefore, the death angel destroyed the first born of the Egyptians but had to spare the first born of the children of Israel.

¹² He went once for all into the [Holy of] Holies [of heaven], not by virtue of the blood of goats and calves [by which to make reconciliation between God and man], but His own blood, having found and secured a complete redemption (an everlasting release for us). (Hebrews 9:12 AMP)

As Christians, we no longer have to apply the blood of animals because Jesus shed His blood for our redemption and forgiveness. Applying this same blood brings healing and protection against every curse that the enemy could ever seek to bring in the life of the believer.

Even today, God has given you divine authority to declare a no-fly zone over your life by **pleading the blood of Jesus** over everything that belongs to you. As you make this declaration in the realm of the spirit no demon will be able to come near your dwelling place.

In other words, demonic assassins cannot infiltrate these areas once you prophetically declare them off limits. With this declaration you stand in a place of kingdom authority as you establish a spiritual force field commanding angelic hosts to stand guard against the enemy on your behalf.

> *9 Because thou hast made the LORD, which is my refuge, even the most High, thy habitation;*
>
> *10 There shall no evil befall thee, neither shall any plague come nigh thy dwelling.*
> *(Psalm 91:9–10)*

God is calling believers to establish no-fly zone areas over their lives, churches, communities, families and regions. As a sharpshooter or intercessor in the Kingdom of God, if the enemy, including witches, demons and the like try to violate these no-fly boundaries you have established in the spirit, you are licensed by the Spirit of God to destroy them.

Witches and demons often use the midnight hour to seek to invade your privacy and sabotage your life. As you intensify your fight at midnight declare that your house, church and business are no-fly zones.

Once you have declared a no-fly zone in the realm of the spirit, you can stand boldly upon your watch tower and oversee matters concerning the Kingdom.

THE WATCH TOWER – AIR TRAFFIC CONTROL

"I have set watchmen upon thy walls, O Jerusalem, which shall never hold their peace day nor night: ye that make mention of the LORD, keep not silence," (Isaiah 62:6)

Air Traffic Control Personnel hold some of the most vital positions in aviation. They are responsible for monitoring and directing the movements of aircrafts in a designated area by communicating with the pilots who are flying the aircrafts. No pilot is allowed to take off or land their aircraft without first communicating with the Air Traffic Control Tower in that region.

The Word of God reveals that God has established watchmen, watchers or lookers in the Body of Christ. These prophetic intercessors are either Prophets, themselves, or have been given instructions from their spiritual leader who operates in the office of the Prophet or Apostle. This group of intercessors functions as Spiritual Air Traffic Controllers. They are called and anointed to stand in watch towers in the realm of the spirit; in order to monitor or observe the spiritual climate of a family, church, region or global community.

Spiritual Air Traffic Controllers also have the ability, through prayer and intercession, to instruct, redirect or shift atmospheres. Further, they have a spiritual mandate to expose deficient moral, social and spiritual values which seek to undermine the principles of the Word of God. God used prophets such as: Moses, Samuel, Jeremiah, Isaiah, Elijah and Elisha to function in similar capacities.

As a prayer warrior when you stand upon your watch you will experience increased levels of spiritual sensitivity and will function in a higher dimension of spiritual authority. Your new dimension of spiritual authority empowers you to take possession of new spiritual domains and territories.

> *"I will stand upon my watch, and set me upon the tower, and will watch to see what he will say unto me, and what I shall answer when I am reproved." (Habakkuk 2:1)*

A TERRITORIAL ANOINTING
"Dispossessing the enemy; possessing and taking hold of territories!"

Throughout the annals of history many military conflicts have taken place between rival nations for the sole purpose of determining who would reign over a specific territory or region. As a sovereign state, every country enacts laws, bylaws, creeds and codes by which it would seek to govern its citizens.

Whenever a group of people or nation wanted to possess new lands, they had to first dispossess their enemy by driving them out of the land or subdue them as slaves or servants.

Once the new territory was conquered, they could then show possession by erecting its national flag, generally on an elevated area such as a hill. In some cities they would build a presidential palace or temple.

This act indicated to all that the ruling nation was staking ownership to the territory and simultaneously making a national declaration that their system of government prevailed there.

"Every place that the sole of your foot shall tread upon, that have I given unto you,..."
(Joshua 1:3)

During spiritual warfare there is an ongoing battle between the unseen forces of good and evil, just as there is a battle between the Kingdom of God and the kingdom of satan. However, the targeted spiritual territory, the prime possession is your mind. Your enemy seeks to gain complete control of your soul, which comprises your mind, will, intellect and emotions.

This is the battleground where the conflict takes place. If the enemy can gain control of your mind, he can manipulate your entire existence and, ultimately, destroy you.

> ***Taking Captivity Of Your Soul***
> ***Brings Captivity To Your Life!***

¹⁰ The thief cometh not, but for to steal, and to kill, and to destroy: I am come that they might have life, and that they might have it more abundantly. (John 10:10)

The enemy not only seeks to gain control of your life, he also seeks to dominate entire families and nations. It is his primary objective to inflict, distress, oppress, abuse and sabotage peoples' lives. In order to win this battle over the enemy, you must cultivate what I call a *territorial anointing*.

"Submit yourselves therefore to God. Resist
the devil, and he will flee from you."
(James 4:7)

In **James 4:7** the Word of God give us the formula for developing a territorial anointing by *resisting* or **dispossessing** the enemy while *submitting to* or **possessing** the things of God in your life. The act of submitting to the will of God while resisting the temptations of the enemy denote that there is some level of struggle or contention involved in gaining new grounds in the realm of the spirit.

You must be prepared to fight and employ every spiritual weapon God has given you, especially the weapons of prayer, declaring the Word of God and the name of Jesus in order to gain and maintain your divine miracles and breakthroughs.

Isaac used his territorial anointing to fight for the wells his father had dug. Every time he dug a new well, his enemies, the Philistines would fill it with dirt, however, Isaac never gave up. He simply dug another well until they left him alone. **(Genesis 26: 1–22)**

If you are going to succeed in any area, you must lay siege of every dimension or territory in the realm of the spirit, through prayer. You decree and declare, in Jesus' name, that every demon spirit operating in that place be subdued, bound and removed. Then you declare that the grounds taken belong to God and you are His representative.

THE POWER OF THE PRAYER WATCHES

To watch means to observe or keep a vigil. A prayer watch is a concentrated period of prayer where believers can come into corporate agreement or where you choose to set aside time to seek the face of God during a 24-hour period. Prayer watches are strategic in nature as intercession is made for specific targets. Jesus, the Chief Intercessor, observed specific times of prayer during His ministry.

There are eight prayer watches mentioned throughout scripture. They occur at specific times of the day or night. The evening is the foundation of the watches so what happens during your night will determine what occurs during the course of your day.

Prayer has also always been an integral part of the custom of the Children of Israel. The Bible speaks about how Daniel prayed, turning his head towards the east three times a day.

In *Acts 3:1* Peter and John went to the Temple at the hour of prayer. In *Matthew 14:25* Jesus, who had just come out of a time of prayer, came walking on the water during the fourth watch of the night.

²⁵ And in the fourth watch of the night Jesus went unto them, walking on the sea.
(Matthew 14:25)

These watches and prayer times were scheduled at specific intervals and were even used to regiment daily schedules and lifestyles.

> ## THE *FIRST* WATCH OF THE NIGHT
> ### *The Watch of Devotion*
> ### (6:00 p.m. to 9:00 p.m.)

This is the gate or opening for the beginning of the new watch of the night. This is the time for the manifestation of the Father. God said in **Matthew 16:16-19** that you must possess the gates. One of the key factors you need in order to do so is the key of knowledge. Before you go into prayer, time should be spent in the Word. You may also include your family devotions time before children go to bed.

SCRIPTURE REFERENCES: Psalm 119: 148; Isaiah 17:12-14; Psalms 59

> ## THE *SECOND* WATCH OF THE NIGHT
> ### *The Watch of Spiritual Preparation*
> ### (9:00 p.m. to Midnight)

This is the time to worship and exalt the Lord. It is the prayer time for those who have been given heavy kingdom mandates from God; servant leaders who are involved in ministries which are on the frontline of battle; or for those who have been called with a specific assignment. It is also time to call on God for divine favor and protection.

SCRIPTURE REFERENCES: 1 Chronicles 16:25–29 Exodus 3:21; Exodus 11:3, 4; Psalm 86:12; Psalm 119:148; Psalm 121:5–8; Deuteronomy 31:8

---

12 MINUTES TO BREAKTHROUGH

> ## THE *THIRD* WATCH OF THE NIGHT
> ### *The Watch of Execution and Breakthrough*
> **(Midnight to 3:00 a.m.)**

This is one of the most important times to keep watch. It is the hour of **prophetic reversal** and the time to wage spiritual warfare against your enemies through the blood of Jesus. The midnight watch is the best time for you to present your case before God in prayer. This watch is also called **the bewitching hour** because this is the time of heightened satanic activity.

This watch of the night is when most witches and people in the realm of darkness engage in demonic activities or bewitchment, séances and other *dark* practices. They seek to increase their activity due to the fact that there is minimal activity in the earth realm because most people, including Christians, are asleep.

This midnight watch is the time for believers to arise out of sleep and confront every demon because God has given us power over all the powers of the enemy.

> *19 Behold, I give unto you power to tread on serpents and scorpions, and over all the power of the enemy: and nothing shall by any means hurt you. (Luke 10:19)*

Praying in this Third Watch will annihilate **all** satanic plans, giving you the victory and manifesting your breakthrough.

SCRIPTURE REFERENCES: Psalm 91; Exodus 12:29; Psalm 119:62

> ## THE *FOURTH* WATCH OF THE NIGHT
> ### *The Watch of Peace and Deliverance*
> ### (3:00 a.m. to 6:00 a.m.)

This watch is referred to as the **Early Morning Watch**. In **Mark 1:35** we see Jesus rising very early to find a solitary place to pray. Prayers during this watch are for the will of God to be established on earth as it has already been established in heaven. This prayer time is also for deliverance, divine judgment and resurrection. It is no longer what you want, but God's divine will that you are seeking.

SCRIPTURE REFERENCES: Isaiah 58:8; Isaiah 50:4; Psalm 5, Job 3:9; Job 22:27–28

> ## THE *FIRST* WATCH OF THE DAY
> ### *The Watch of Expectation*
> ### (6:00 a.m. to 9:00 a.m.)

This is the watch for the beginning of sunrise and it is time to pray for healing, power and outpouring of Holy Spirit. During this prayer watch of the day you rise up with spiritual boldness and confidence to speak life into your day with declarations and utterances according to the Word of God. It is the dawning of a brand new day filled with joy and great expectations.

SCRIPTURE REFERENCES: Acts 2:4; Habakkuk 2:1

---

12 MINUTES TO BREAKTHROUGH

> ## THE *SECOND* WATCH OF THE DAY
> ### *The Watch of Recommitment and Dedication*
> ### (9:00 a.m. to 12 noon)

According to **Matthew 20:3**, you are considered idle if you have not started working by the beginning of this watch. It is required that during this watch you remain spiritually active and focused on fulfilling God's purpose in your life for every moment of the day. It is the time to recommit yourself to the leading of Holy Spirit. You have already started your personal routine for that day, but know that the outcome of your day will depend solely on your dedication to the will and work of God.

SCRIPTURE REFERENCES: 1 Kings 8:56, Joshua 23:14; Matthew 20:3, Galatians 2:20, Colossians 3:5

> ## THE *THIRD* WATCH OF THE DAY
> ### *The Watch of Release and Victory*
> ### (12 noon to 3 p.m.)

This is the watch to exercise your dominion as a child of God because this is the time that the promises of God are released and God is shaking the foundations of the wicked. Christ became the atonement for our sins, during this time.

Therefore, you move in this watch with absolute dominion, power and authority. This is also the time to dwell in the secret place of God while declaring the Word of God over your daily experiences. Concentrated prayer during this watch will activate a *Season of Release* in your life as you remain confident in the Lord, God Almighty.

¹ At the end of every seven years thou shalt make a release.

² And this is the manner of the release: Every creditor that lendeth ought unto his neighbour shall release it; he shall not exact it of his neighbour, or of his brother; because it is called the LORD's release.

³ Of a foreigner thou mayest exact it again: but that which is thine with thy brother thine hand shall release;

⁴ Save when there shall be no poor among you; for the LORD shall greatly bless thee in the land which the LORD thy God giveth thee for an inheritance to possess it:

⁵ Only if thou carefully hearken unto the voice of the LORD thy God, to observe to do all these commandments which I command thee this day.

⁶ For the LORD thy God blesseth thee, as he promised thee: and thou shalt lend unto many nations, but thou shalt not borrow; and thou shalt reign over many nations, but they shall not reign over thee.
(Deuteronomy 15:1–6)

² And he is the propitiation for our sins: and not for ours only, but also for the sins of the whole world. (1 John 2:2)

This is often referred to as the **Time of Release** and the time stand on the promises of God while speaking the Word of God over every area in your life. *(Psalm 91)*

SCRIPTURE REFERENCES: Psalms 37:20; Psalm 91; Matthew 27:45; Deuteronomy 15:1-6; 1 John 2:2

THE *FOURTH* WATCH OF THE DAY
The Watch of Prayer, Praise and Power
(3:00 p.m. to 6:00 p.m.)

According to the Word of God this is the last watch of the day and ushers in the **Hour of Prayer** as recorded in **Acts 3:1 and Acts 10:3**. The most important privilege of the entire church is prayer.

This is also the time God shaped history because it is believed that this is the watch during which Jesus died on the cross. History changed forever when Jesus died because He triumphed over death, hell and the grave to become the mediator of our Blood Covenant with God. This watch brings spiritual authority and power that will cause history to change in your favor as you are pushed towards your divine destiny.

SCRIPTURE REFERENCES: Matthew 27:45-46; Luke 23:44-46; Acts 3:1; Acts 10:3, Acts 10:30-32

God is a God of War. In this office of military might, He is known as Jehovah Gibbor. He is the consummate military strategist who is not intimidated by confrontation but has faced, fought and won every battle for His people. He has, in turn, equipped every believer with the spiritual artillery necessary to win at every level of spiritual warfare. The more you engage your spiritual weapons, especially prayer, the greater the victories you will begin to experience.

CHAPTER TEN

12 MINUTES TO
BREAKTHROUGH

WHAT IS 12 MINUTES TO BREAKTHROUGH?

The *12 Minutes To Breakthrough Prayer Strategy* is a powerful, effective prayer weapon of mass destruction for use against the enemy. It helps the believer to learn and engage kingdom tactics to overcome difficult and adverse situations.

This powerful prayer strategy is designed to break you through to your next level of glorious victory once and for all, affording you the opportunity to begin enjoying the abundant life that Father God has reserved for you *(John 10:10).*

If you find yourself or your family in a perpetual cycle of dealing with *stubborn problems* which will not seem to go away, or they go away only to return a few seasons later, then this *12 Minutes to Breakthrough Prayer Routine* is designed to give you the spiritual fortitude necessary to gain absolute victory.

Moreover, *12 Minutes to Breakthrough* is a practical strategy that teaches you prayer principles during spiritual warfare on how to gain the victory against your enemy. This powerful weapon is designed to combat every demonic plan that may be formed against you. It is the believer's secret weapon that gives ultimate victory in every area of life.

This *12 Minutes To Breakthrough Prayer Strategy* is a prophetic declaration and divine activation. It makes a declarative statement to the gates of hell that you are not giving up and you are now engaged in the divine conflict.

Holy Spirit released this prayer strategy to me and said that this will help those who are faced with **stubborn problems** and are on the brink of a miracle or the brink of their breakthrough.

WHO SHOULD ENGAGE THIS 12 MINUTES TO BREAKTHROUGH STRATEGY?

The 12 Minutes To Breakthrough Prayer Strategy is for every believer, especially those who may be called to serve in ministry such as: *apostles, prophets, teachers, evangelists, armourbearers, intercessors, musicians, security personnel, publications & media personnel, youth & children's leaders and more.*

Every person working in ministry should know how to engage this powerful *Prayer Strategy.* It is a proven fact that no matter what area of ministry you are called to work in, you will need to know how to pray. However, the enemy specifically targets you if you are in the frontline of leadership and he may even use or attack you if you are on the sidelines.

I have seen so many unnecessary casualties in ministry which could have been avoided if only someone had known how to pray strategically.

Many pastors are attacked and some ultimately succumb to the onslaught of the enemy, abandon their calling and give up on their ministry. These casualties occur due to the fact that their support and prayer covering from armourbearers and intercessors become weakened.

In **Exodus 17**, as Aaron and Hur held up the hands of Moses, the Children of Israel won the battle. When Moses' hands fell, Israel lost the battle.

Therefore, as a spiritual leader, if you are going to win your battles on the frontline, not only do you need to know how to fight in prayer, the people who you surround yourself with must also know how to win during times of spiritual warfare.

> ***Once The Breakthrough Manifests In The Realm Of The Spirit, It Is Mandated To Manifest In The Natural Realm.***

WHEN TO ENGAGE THIS 12 MINUTES TO BREAKTHROUGH STRATEGY?

You will know that you need to use the 12 minutes to breakthrough strategy when you feel as if you are under a demonic attack of the enemy in some area of your life; namely:

1) If you are experiencing chronic cycles of poverty and lack or are having repeated financial hardships and have difficulties paying your bills

- You feeling as if money is slipping through your hands
- You are constantly feeling as if you are coming up short at the end of each month
- You constantly finding yourself in a financial bind
- You having to keep borrowing to pay others

2) If you or your loved ones are experiencing unexplainable sicknesses, diseases or disorders

- You finding that the doctors cannot diagnose what is going on in your body
- Various unexpected abnormalities in your body
- You are afflicted with constant diseases or illnesses common to your family members
- You having to endure long periods of taking medication

3) If you are experiencing unexplainable tragedies or dilemmas

- You are enduring continual cycles of rejection
- You are constantly facing persistent failure and defeat
- You are constantly being told "No!" or are turned away from opportunities for no reason.

4) If everything keeps dying or breaking down around you or if you continue to experience repetitive loss, failure or disappointment

- Your car or other electronic devices continually malfunction for no reason.
- There are repeated tragedies or untimely deaths occurring in your family
- You are qualified for a position or contract but you are not receiving it
- You keep missing or losing opportunities you know were given to you by God

5) If you or someone you love is constantly experiencing repetitive cycles of disunity and disagreements in the family or marriage and other relationships

- You are living or working in a perpetually hostile environment
- You and your spouse are communicating with constant contention and confrontation
- Your children are insistently disobedient and rebellious toward their parents
- Family events which should be happy constantly end with everyone in derision and confusion

6) If your dreams are sometimes overshadowed by demonic activities, such as:
- Nightmares or feelings of torment
- You having repetitive dreams that you are being shot at
- You seeing your hair being cut in your dream
- You finding yourself constantly surrounded by animals such as snakes, dogs, rats, spiders, insects or being bitten by them in your dreams
- You having repetitive dreams that you are falling from a tall building or down a mountain
- You having repetitive dreams that you are swimming in dirty waters or in waters surrounded by sharks
- You dreaming that you are drowning or being suffocated
- You feeling as if you have had sex in your dream
- You feeling as if you have been bitten in your dream
- You constantly driving to dead ends or in a circle
- Doors slamming closed in your face
- You are standing on trial in a courtroom and they are wrongfully accusing and sentencing you

- You dreaming that you or a loved one is in a grave or coffin
- You being married in your dream and you have no knowledge of the person you are marrying.

WHY ENGAGE THIS 12 MINUTES TO BREAKTHROUGH STRATEGY?

As a warrior in Christ, it is almost guaranteed that the more you become skilled in spiritual warfare, the greater chances you will have to return home alive after the battle is over. Therefore, as a believer you must learn to fight the good fight of faith and gain insight at every level of conflict.

In **Ephesians 6:10** Paul admonishes every believer to put on the whole armor of God so that you are able to stand against the wiles of the devil.

> *10 Finally, my brethren, be strong in the Lord, and in the power of his might.*
>
> *11 Put on the whole armour of God, that ye may be able to stand against the wiles of the devil.*
>
> *12 For we wrestle not against flesh and blood, but against principalities, against powers, against the rulers of the darkness of this world, against spiritual wickedness in high places.*
> *(Ephesians 6:10 – 12)*

Further, this scripture indicates that satan has established a highly organized demonic hierarchy in an effort to keep the life of every believer in bondage, oppression and defeat. It is these and other demonic influences from which you must radically break free during the *12 Minutes to Breakthrough Prayer Strategy.*

THE BENEFITS OF PRAYER

The *12 Minutes to Breakthrough Strategy* is designed to accomplish specific and definite results. This powerful prayer tactic produces immediate results in the spirit. When anything happens in the spirit realm it is mandated to manifest in the natural realm.

As you diligently seek God you will discover that this life-changing breakthrough prayer strategy will ACTIVATE numerous spiritual victories in your life. Additionally, as you PRAY, you can be confident that your:

- Prayer produces power.
- Prayer opens divine portals.
- Prayer activates angels.
- Prayer provides divine protection and unlocks the supernatural, causing you to see in the invisible realm; angels are at your beck and call.
- Prayer causes the glory of God to be manifested and revealed.
- Prayer causes the glory of God to be sustained and maintained in your life.
- Prayer activates the anointing on your life.
- Prayer demands answers.
- Prayer causes the oil from heaven to flow.
- Prayer ignites the fire of the Holy Ghost in your life.
- Prayer releases divine revelation from God.

- Prayer activates the anointing on your life.
- Prayer effects positive change in you and in the life of your family.
- Prayer destroys every yoke.
- Prayer shuts down satanic surveillances and blocks demonic gateways to your mind and soul.
- Prayer releases blindness upon your enemies so they cannot detect your movements.
- Prayer shuts down demonic surveillances so that they can no longer hear your conversations.
- Prayer weakens and destroys your enemy's resistance and causes you to push through the hard places.
- Prayer produces resilience and stimulates tenacity.
- Prayer helps to fortify your faith.
- Prayer brings divine restoration; everything lost is returned to you a hundredfold.
- Prayer destroys the destroyer, including witches, warlocks and wicked people as well as *spiritual locusts* and *caterpillars* which have sought to devour your life.
- Prayer crushes the head of the serpent and totally annihilates the workings of this demonic adversary.
- Prayer causes you to sharpen your spiritual weaponry and transforms you into a skilled warrior.
- Prayer breaks the arrows that fly by day; disables destruction at noonday; eradicates pestilence by night.
- Prayer vindicates the righteous.
- Prayer lets the oppressed go free.
- Prayer gives you beauty for ashes, the oil of joy for gladness and a garment of praise instead of mourning.

- Prayer becomes a shield and buckler.
- Prayer sharpens your sword and gives powerful, spiritual discernment.
- Prayer gives revelation, illumination and divine impartation.
- Prayer casts out demonic spirits of fear, pride and doubt.
- Prayer produces humility, holiness and love. It creates new doors of opportunity, causing windows and portals of heaven to open.
- Prayer causes healing, deliverance and produces miracles, signs and wonders.
- Prayer raises the dead.
- Prayer beats down lies and causes the spirit of truth and honesty to prevail.
- Prayer silences commotion and brings peace.
- Prayer fosters a spirit of gratitude.
- Prayer honors God and exalts the name of Jesus.

The **12 Minutes To Breakthrough Prayer Strategy** is a powerful weapon in the hands of believers who see God as their only source and are determined to effect change in their lives. You must be prepared to consistently implement this strategy and watch the Spirit of God move miraculously on your behalf.

CHAPTER ELEVEN

PREPARING FOR YOUR

BREAKTHROUGH

PREPARING FOR YOUR BREAKTHROUGH

The *12 Minutes to Breakthrough Prayer Strategy* is designed to help you gain absolute victory in every area of your life, especially **U.R.G.E.N.T.,** persistent matters which have come to challenge you, your family, business, ministry or any area in your life. *Whenever you are faced with an U.R.G.E.N.T. matter, this simply means that you are in a spiritual dilemma and are:*

U – Unwilling to wait another minute

R – Ready for my miracle

G – Getting tired of this problem

E – Engaging my battle

N – Needing to move now

T – Time to take immediate action

As you engage this strategy you will pray *for 12 days at 12 noon and 12 midnight every day for 12 minutes minimum.* This **12** day routine can be repeated as often as you desire over a **12** week or a **12** month period. This strategy can be implemented by an individual, family, group or church.

Here Is How It Is Done...

- Start by **setting aside 12 days** that you can engage in strategic prayer.

- **Take a pen and paper and write down the 12 most urgent things that you need to pray for**. If you have less than **12**, that is fine. Then write them big and bold enough for you to read them from a distance.

- **Create a prayer wall** or build a small billboard area where you can post your prayer requests.

- Then **print out 12 scripture verses that are related to your prayer needs** or you can choose to use the scriptures which are given in this chapter. You can post them on the prayer wall as well.

- If you have photos of yourself, the person or place you are praying for, these can also be **posted on the prayer wall.**

- **Prepare to journal your experiences.** It will be beneficial to keep a journal of your daily routine and record your entire experience. Take notes of whatever Holy Spirit speaks to your heart. Write down every dream or vision you have during this season of prayer as the Spirit of God uses many ways to point you to your breakthrough. *(See my book, "I Still Want You!" pg. 64 on Interpretive Signs and Wonders in the Chapter entitled, "Hearing The Voice of God!")*

12 MINUTES TO BREAKTHROUGH DAILY WORKOUT ROUTINE

As your Prayer Strategy Coach I submit to you the following daily routine which, when followed, will break you through to your next level in strategic prayer and manifesting the things of God.

One of the most exciting things about this routine is that it is always relevant and never loses its validity. In other words, you can utilize this strategy whenever you are faced with any challenging situation, discouraging dilemma or vexing issue.

You can also implement this strategy if you just need a breakthrough in prayer or want to experience more of the presence of God. This prayer strategy can be utilized at any time, any day or during any season of your life. You can have **12** days of prayer, **12** weeks of prayer or even **12** months of prayer using the same routine.

STEPS ON HOW TO PREPRARE FOR YOUR 12 MINUTES TO BREAKTHROUGH ROUTINE

- **Consecrate and Set Aside a Place for Prayer** – as your battleground. If it is in your home, choose an area you can call your battle room. Build an altar, place your Bible on it, spray the ENGEDI WATER or Oil upon your head and hands or throughout the room, if needed; place your prayer list on your prayer cloth which can also represent your altar. If you are using the Church, then there is already an altar in place.

- **Begin On Day One By Declaring a 1-Day Fast** - In order to effectively engage in the *12 Minutes To Breakthrough Daily Routine* you must spiritually prepare yourself for this encounter. You can begin on the first day by placing a sacrificial fast on the altar before the Lord.

  What is fasting? Fasting is the abstaining from food or anything that is pleasurable for a period of time for spiritual edification, cleansing and deliverance. Fasting places your flesh under subjection while your spiritual man is quickened or made alive to the things of God. This fast may be similar to a Daniel Fast where you abstain from all meats, sweets, etc. However, you may choose to eat fruits, vegetables, salads, nuts, and drink lots of purified water.

  ⁶ Is not this the fast that I have chosen? to loose the bands of wickedness, to undo the heavy burdens, and to let the oppressed go free, and that ye break every yoke? (Isaiah 58:6)

- **Set Your Clock and Mark Your Time For Prayer** – Begin to make specific and deliberate preparations for entering the presence of God. Set your alarm clock at least five minutes before the midnight hour. This will alert you to begin your preparations to enter His presence.

- **Settle Your Spirit** – Begin to quiet your surroundings; discontinue your scheduled activities; turn your television and cell phone off; remove yourself from anything that would seek to distract you from the next **12** crucial minutes.

- **Set The Atmosphere** – You set the atmosphere with worship music, you remove your shoes as a sign of humility and reverence as you prepare to enter the presence of your king. Begin to make your way to your designated threshing floor, your secret place, the place you have sanctified and hallowed to meet and petition your King.

- **Remove your shoes** – During biblical times, shoes were a sign of status, economic power, notoriety and wealth. Removing your shoes is a sign of humility; you strip yourself of everything that brings glory to yourself as you reverence the presence of the Lord. *(Joshua 5:15)*

- **Layout your 12 Minutes to Breakthrough Prayer Mat** – Lay your mat out on the floor so that at the end of your *12 Minutes Routine* you can lay before the Lord to hear His voice or receive instructions. You may be given a dream, strong impression or even see visions. Rest in the Lord and wait patiently for Him, then spiritual portals will open to you.

- **Anoint or spray your head** with the Anointed **ENGEDI WATER** for Breakthrough or apply it to the area where needed. The water releases a fresh anointing on your life. If there is need for deliverance, you will immediately begin to experience it. *(See the back of this book for more information about the Engedi Breakthrough and Deliverance Water)*

- **Recite the scriptures for the day.** The Word of God is further activated when you declare it with your own tongue. The clock now strikes midnight and you can employ the *12 Minutes to Breakthrough Strategy* of militant prayer.

Continue to Worship and Pray in the Spirit (Pray in Tongues)

When the Spirit of God gave me this *12 Minutes To Breakthrough Strategy* He told me that if I prayed in the Spirit I would see instant miracles.

"...but the Spirit itself maketh intercession for us with groanings which cannot be uttered."
(Romans 8:26)

As you pray in the Spirit for at least **12** minutes twice daily I believe that you will receive immediate results. If you need to be filled with Holy Spirit with the evidence of speaking in tongues, please pray this simple prayer, in faith, and allow Holy Spirit to baptize you afresh.

PRAY THIS PRAYER FOR BAPTISM IN THE HOLY SPIRIT

PRAYER: *Father God, I worship you and I give you all the glory and praise for what you are doing in my life. Thank you for allowing Jesus Christ to die on the Cross for my sins. I am a born again believer and would like to be baptized in the Holy Spirit. Holy Spirit fill me right now and cause me to speak in other tongues. I receive this gift now, by faith, and as I open my mouth speak through me, in Jesus' name.*

Now open your mouth and begin speaking in tongues, the heavenly language you hear in your spirit. Do not speak your native language. Although the tongue may sound foreign to you, speak whatever Holy Spirit drops into your spirit. The more you speak, the more you will be activated to do so and your heavenly language will begin to flow out of you like a fountain of living waters.

38 He that believeth on me, as the scripture hath said, out of his belly shall flow rivers of living water. (John 7:38)

CHAPTER TWELVE

YOUR 12 MINUTES TO BREAKTHROUGH PRAYER STRATEGY

YOUR BREAKTHROUGH BEGINS HERE!

THE 12-DAY-TO-DAY PRAYER ROUTINE FOR 12 MINUTES AT 12 NOON AND 12 MIDNIGHT

THIS IS YOUR 12 DAY SPIRITUAL WARFARE AND PRAYER STRATEGY

PLEASE NOTE

Begin Each Day By Praying In The Spirit. Then Quote The Word Of God Related To Your Prayer Focus. You Are Not Limited To Only Quoting The Scriptures Given In The Following 12 Minutes To Breakthrough Day-To-Day Strategy. You Can Employ As Many Scriptures As You Desire, Especially Ones That Directly Combat The Situation You Are Going Through.

DAY #1: PREPARE FOR HIS PRESENCE...IT'S TIME TO SEEK HIM!

This is the first day of your Breakthrough Prayer Routine. Therefore, you must set the precedence for your day and command your morning as you seek the Lord early.

#PreparingForHisPresence

READ THIS PRAYER IN FAITH AND BELIEVE GOD TO MANIFEST YOUR BREAKTHROUGH:

Father in the name of Jesus, You are my God, and I have come to seek You and only You for the answers I need in this season of my life. I am desperate for a word from You, my soul thirst for You; my flesh longs for You in this barren place in which I find myself. As I look all around me, I see that you are my only Source, there is no one that can do for me what you can. I find no rest or peace in anything or anyone but in Your presence, O Lord! Your Word says that in your presence there is fullness of joy and at your right hand there are pleasures forevermore. You are my joy, O Lord. You are my peace and You have become my song.

Now create in me a clean heart, O God and renew the right spirit within me. Take away anything in me that is not like You or pleasing in Your sight. Cleanse me from all unrighteousness and cover me with your grace, that I may be clean in your sight. Remove every attitude, belief or carnal mindset that would hinder me from hearing and interpreting your voice. I need you Jesus and I believe that if I seek I shall find you.

Lord, God Jehovah You are my God of Breakthrough so I ask in the name of Jesus that you send your angel called Breakthrough to fight on my behalf. I am in urgent need of help. So right now I call on Angel Breakthrough. Angel Breakthrough come now in the strength of the Lord and cause me to triumph over mine enemies.

You are my God, my Savior and my Deliverer...according to your loving kindness hear me when I cry with my voice and answer me, O Lord....in Jesus name I pray! AMEN!

SCRIPTURE REFERENCES:

O God, thou art my God; early will I seek thee: my soul thirsteth for thee, my flesh longeth for thee in a dry and thirsty land, where no water is; My soul thirsteth for thee in a dry and thirsty land where no water is.
(Psalms 63:1)

Create in me a clean heart, O God; and renew a right spirit within me. **(Psalm 51:10)**

But if from thence thou shalt seek the LORD thy God, thou shalt find [him], if thou seek him with all thy heart and with all thy soul. **(Deuteronomy 4:29)**

"...in thy presence is fulness of joy; at thy right hand there are pleasures for evermore." **(Psalm 16:11b)**

DAY #2: COME IN AGREEMENT WITH HOLY SPIRIT AND BECOME HUNGRY FOR HIM

As you continue to seek Him, you become more desperate and hungry for Him. You soon begin to realize that only Christ can satisfy and fill every need and void in your life.

#DesperateForHim

READ THIS PRAYER IN FAITH AND BELIEVE GOD TO MANIFEST YOUR BREAKTHROUGH:

Father God, in the name of Jesus, I acknowledge that you are the Alpha and the Omega. You are the beginning and the ending. You are the first and the last. You are the Author and the Finisher of my faith. I believe that You are my source for all things and I worship You. I love You Lord because You first loved me. You said in Your Word that according to Your Divine Power that You have given me everything I need to live an acceptable life before you. You gave us Jesus, and I believe that because of Him that You will continue to bless me in this life and with Your presence.

I am grateful for everything that You have done for me. I am saved because of Your grace and now I ask that You would overshadow my life. I come in agreement with Your will and purpose for my life. God I need You more than I need anything else. I am alive today because You loved me; You sacrificed for me; You comforted me and You preserved my life. Father, I am lost without You!

12 MINUTES TO BREAKTHROUGH

I am desperate for You! I need you Lord to fill every void in my life, mend my brokenness, heal my hurts and fill me with Your presence. I Love You Lord, more than anything else in this world. In Jesus name I pray! AMEN!

Are You Ready For Your Breakthrough?

SCRIPTURE REFERENCES:

According as his divine power hath given unto us all things that pertain unto life and godliness, through the knowledge of him that hath called us to glory and virtue:
(2 Peter 1:3)

He who did not withhold or spare [even] His own Son but gave Him up for us all, will He not also with Him freely and graciously give us all [other] things?
(Romans 8:32)

Again I say unto you, That if two of you shall agree on earth as touching any thing that they shall ask, it shall be done for them of my Father which is in heaven.
(Matthew 18:19)

Blessed are they which do hunger and thirst after righteousness: for they shall be filled.
(Matthew 5:6)

Serve the LORD with gladness: come before his presence with singing.
(Psalm 100:2)

DAY #3: SURRENDER BODY, SOUL AND SPIRIT TO THE WILL OF ALMIGHTY GOD

As you pray in the Holy Ghost or pray in tongues, before the Lord, your carnal man is weakened as your spirit man increases or becomes strengthened to prophetically declare the will of God in your situation; your body, soul and spirit submits to the leading of Holy Spirit.

#ISurrenderAll

READ THIS PRAYER IN FAITH AND BELIEVE GOD TO MANIFEST YOUR BREAKTHROUGH:

Father God, in the name of Jesus I come before Your throne because I believe that You are my God and beside You there is no other. I thank you because Your Word declares that the plans You have for me are to prosper me; to give me hope and something to look forward to. I trust Your Word, O Lord! I trust You Lord!

You are my shield and strength and my life is in Your hands, O Lord. I yield my will to Your Word, I yield my thoughts to Your thoughts; I yield my mind to Your mind and take on the mind of Christ and I do not depend on my own thoughts, reasonings and understandings; for Your ways are not my ways and neither are your thoughts my thoughts.

Father as I yield myself, more and more to Your will I pray that You would fill me with Your spirit. Overshadow me with Your grace so that I will speak Your thoughts, Your Words and Your will concerning my situation. I release every concern to You. I lay them at your feet and ask that You send answers now from your Throne Room. In Jesus name I pray! AMEN!

Your Breakthrough Is Here!

SCRIPTURE REFERENCES:

Trust in the Lord with all thine heart; and lean not unto thine own understanding. [6] In all thy ways acknowledge him, and he shall direct thy paths.
(Proverbs 3: 5, 6)

*And they were all filled with the Holy Ghost, and began to speak with other tongues, as the Spirit gave them utterance. **(Acts 2:4)***

*"And when Paul had laid his hands upon them, the Holy Ghost came on them; and they spake with tongues, and prophesied." **(Acts 19:6)***

DAY #4: SPIRITUAL DISCERNMENT ENABLES YOU TO MARCH AND GO FORTH IN POWER

Once you become empowered and continue to build momentum in the realm of the spirit, you can then develop and implement your battle strategy as you set a watch against your enemy.

#MarchingIntoBattle

READ THIS PRAYER IN FAITH AND BELIEVE GOD TO MANIFEST YOUR BREAKTHROUGH:

Father God, in the name of Jesus, You are the Mighty God; You are the King of Kings and the Lord of Lords. You Are Jehovah Gibbor, the Mighty Warrior who has given me victory over and over again. Father, You are the One who calms all my fears and heals all my diseases. You sent Your Word and healed the diseases of Your people. You are the mighty God who teaches Your people how to do battle. You teach my hands to do warfare and my fingers how to fight.

As Your people approached the battle, they marched towards the enemy. I pray for spiritual strength and fortitude to continue to endure until You send the answer to my dilemma. Father, I set myself to seek You as I set a watch against every attack of the enemy. Show me the way that I should take. Give me the right strategy in this fight to win this battle. Teach me the right way and show me the way to victory. In Jesus name I pray! AMEN!

Your Breakthrough Is In The Finish!
Keep Pushing!

SCRIPTURE REFERENCES:

And it shall be, when thou shalt hear a sound of going
in the tops of the mulberry trees, that then thou shalt
go out to battle: for God has gone forth before thee, to
smite the host of the Philistines."
(1 Chronicles 14:15)

LORD, when thou went out of Seir, when thou marched
out of the field of Edom, the earth trembled, and the
heavens dropped, the clouds also dropped water."
(Judges 5:4)

Nevertheless we made our prayer unto our God, and set a
watch against them day and night, because of them.
(Nehemiah 4:9)

The Lord shall go forth as a mighty man, he shall stir up
jealousy like a man of war: he shall cry, yea, roar; he shall
prevail against his enemies.
(Isaiah 42:13)

DAY #5: EMPLOY THE BATTLE AXE STRATEGY

You are almost halfway through your routine. Be encouraged, you have come this far by the grace of God and He will continue to give you the grace to wage war and fight until you have gained your breakthrough.

#GodIsUsingMeAsHisBattleaxe

READ THIS PRAYER IN FAITH AND BELIEVE GOD TO MANIFEST YOUR BREAKTHROUGH:

Father God, in the name of Jesus, I stand before You to continually give You all praise and glory. I lift up my voice and bless Your name. I declare that You are my righteous banner and by You I will run through troops and leap over walls. I believe that You will give me grace to fight in this battle. I believe that the victory is already won. Make me a battleaxe and a weapon of war through Your Word. Give me the words of power to totally destroy every plan of the enemy against my life.

Release a treading anointing upon me so that I can gain grounds in the realm of the spirit. Teach me to do war, O Lord in the name of Jesus. I claim new levels, new realms and new dimensions in You. Anoint me to do war in this battle, O Lord; tread down my enemies and give me victory....in Jesus name I pray! AMEN!

12 MINUTES TO BREAKTHROUGH

Pushing In Prayer Brings Your Breakthrough!

SCRIPTURE REFERENCES:

Let us therefore come boldly unto the throne of grace, that we may obtain mercy, and find grace to help in time of need.
(Hebrews 4:16)

Thou art my battle axe and weapons of war: for with thee will I break in pieces the nations, and with thee will I destroy kingdoms;
(Jeremiah 51:20)

Through God we shall do valiantly: for it is He that shall tread down our enemies ***(Psalm 60:12)***

For by thee I have run through a troop; and by my God have I leaped over a wall. ***(Psalm 18:29)***

DAY #6:   INTENSIFY YOUR SPIRITUAL LANGUAGE

Life and death is in the power of your tongue. As you speak in your spiritual tongue, you continue to come in agreement with the Spirit of God for your situation. Your mouth is a weapon. Your tongues are spiritual ammunition against your enemy.   Use them to help you gain the victory.

#TonguePower

READ THIS PRAYER IN FAITH AND BELIEVE GOD TO MANIFEST YOUR BREAKTHROUGH:

Father God, in the name of Jesus, I thank You for Your Word. You have declared that life and death is in the power of my tongue. You said that You have given me power over all the powers of the enemy and nothing shall by any means harm me. I come in agreement with Your Word and continue to declare that every weapon formed against me shall not prosper and every tongue that rises against me in judgment, You, O Lord have already condemned.

- *I decree and declare that I am blessed and highly favored of the Lord!*

- *I decree and declare that I shall live and not die!*

- *I decree and declare that I shall overcome every adversary in Jesus name!*

- *I decree and declare that I am above only and not beneath.*

- *I decree and declare that whatsoever I set my hands to do shall prosper in the name of Jesus.*

- *I decree and declare that I am more than a conqueror through the blood of Jesus Christ.*

- *I decree and declare that greater is He that is in me than he that is in the world.*

- *I decree and declare that by faith I shall overcome all things.*

- *I decree and declare that only the wisdom and counsel of the Lord shall stand and that I am blessed going out and I am blessed coming in.*

- *I decree and declare that I have the victory today and that I am more than a conqueror through the blood of Jesus Christ....I pray this prayer in the mighty name of Jesus! AMEN!*

Declare Your Breakthrough!

SCRIPTURE REFERENCES:

Death and life are in the power of the tongue: and they that love it shall eat the fruit thereof.
(Proverbs 18:21)

I called upon the Lord in distress: the Lord answered me, and set me in a large place. ***(Psalms 118:5)***

...because that for this thing the LORD thy God shall bless thee in all thy works, and in all that thou puttest thine hand unto.
(Deuteronomy 15:10b)

For whosoever shall call upon the name of the Lord shall be saved. ***(Romans 10:13)***

...because greater is he that is in you, than he that is in the world. ***(1 John4:4b)***

My counsel shall stand, and I will do my pleasure
(Isaiah 46:10b)

Nay, in all these things we are more than conquerors through him that loved us.
(Romans 8:37)

DAY #7: EMPLOY THE BATTERING RAM STRATEGY...STORM THE GATES!

Continue to be persistent and intensify your prayer. God is giving you strength for the battle. As you continue your pursuit in the realm of the spirit for your breakthrough, God will continue to empower you to overcome your enemy.

#StormingTheGates

READ THIS PRAYER IN FAITH AND BELIEVE GOD TO MANIFEST YOUR BREAKTHROUGH:

Father God, in the name of Jesus, I receive that this battle belongs to you. I decree and declare that I am a Kingdom Warrior; dressed and ready for battle. I decree and declare that today is a day of victory! I decree that today You have girded me with strength for this battle! I decree and declare that today my enemies are subdued under me because You have strengthened and empowered me and connected me, in the realm of the spirit with other kingdom warriors.

Today is the day that I unify with others in the Body of Christ and pray until our breakthrough manifests. I decree and declare that even as the Spirit of the Lord turned Job's captivity after he prayed for his friends, I pray O Lord that You would turn my captivity. I pray that You would turn this situation in my favor and grant me the victory this day.

As a citizen of the Kingdom of God I unite in the realm of the spirit with other prayer warriors and intercessors and we come in agreement with believers everywhere. I pray that prayer warriors and intercessors are locating my need in the realm of the spirit and, as a battering ram I release this prayer in the atmosphere and connect with the faith of other kingdom warriors that we have the victory over every onslaught or attack of the enemy. In the mighty name of Jesus! AMEN!

Radical Prayer Brings Breakthrough!

SCRIPTURE REFERENCES:

"For by thee I have run through a troop; and by my God have I leaped over a wall."
(Psalm 18:29)

For thou hast girded me with strength unto the battle: thou hast subdued under me those that rose up against me. **(Psalms 18:39)**

"...the battle is the Lord's."
(2 Chronicles 20:15)

"The breaker is come up before them:..."
(Micah 2:13)

DAY #8: INTENSIFY YOUR WARFARE...EVERY DEMONIC WALL IS COMING DOWN!

Shout! Shout! Shout! Lift your voice and release a shout. As you make a noise, this invokes angelic assistance on your behalf and every demonic barrier comes down supernaturally.

#ShoutShoutShout

READ THIS PRAYER IN FAITH AND BELIEVE GOD TO MANIFEST YOUR BREAKTHROUGH:

Father God, in the name of Jesus, I lift my voice with a shout and decree and declare that I have the victory in the mighty name of Jesus. I pray that this prayer would open a divine portal of power over me right now, in the name of Jesus. I release Your war angels to fight on my behalf right now. I release angels to war against every demonic prince that has set up a resistance against me right now in the name of Jesus.

I decree and declare that Jesus is my righteous banner and that with Him I have triumphed over my enemies today. I pray that You would release a fire anointing upon my life to break through every demonic barrier in the name of Jesus. I send Michael, the warring prince to warfare against every principality that has sought to stop or block me in the name of Jesus. I intensify in prayer with other prayer warriors and intercessors and break through demonic hindrances in the name of Jesus.

I decree and declare the victory over the warfare in the heavenlies and pray that my answer manifests speedily here in the earth. I thank You for giving me a conqueror's anointing and empowering me with angelic assistance to storm every demonic gate and break through to a greater realm of blessing and glory. I pray this prayer in the mighty name of Jesus! AMEN!

Breakthrough To Your Victory!

SCRIPTURE REFERENCES:

And it came to pass at the seventh time, when the priests blew with the trumpets, Joshua said unto the people, Shout; for the LORD hath given you the city. ***(Joshua 6:16)***

"So the people shouted when the priests blew with the trumpets: and it came to pass, when the people heard the sound of the trumpet, and the people shouted with a great shout, that the wall fell down flat, so that the people went up into the city, every man straight before him, and they took the city."
(Joshua 6:20)

And there was war in heaven: Michael and his angels fought against the dragon...
(Revelation 7:9)

DAY #9: BREAK THROUGH INTO THE SUPERNATURAL REALM BY DECLARING THE WORD

The angels of the Lord are activated to operate on your behalf as you declare the Word of God. Supernatural miracles, signs and wonders occur as the Word of God is spoken with power and authority.

#SupernaturalMiraclesSignsAndWonders

READ THIS PRAYER IN FAITH AND BELIEVE GOD TO MANIFEST YOUR BREAKTHROUGH:

Father God, in the name of Jesus, even as I have broken through into the realm of God, I decree and declare that You are the God of the supernatural in my life. I believe that in the realm of God that all things are possible. I decree that miracles, signs and wonders are your handiwork and that You are the God of miracles. I believe that One Word from You can change my life forever.

I thank You that You uphold all things by the Word of Your power and by the power of Your Word. I esteem You as the El Elyon, the Mighty God. The One who exists in a category all by Yourself. I pray for a Supernatural release from the realm of the spirit and that You would manifest your divine presence on my behalf right now. I believe that at Your Word, You can release a Kairos moment on my behalf. Release it to me now O Lord. I pray that the fullness of Your will be done and that Your kingdom would come to me now; send wisdom, send power, send knowledge

and understanding, send revelation in Your Word, send Your divine counsel manifest Your glory in my life through this situation and I will forever give you all glory, honor and praise. pray this prayer in Jesus name! AMEN!

Breakthrough To The Supernatural Realm of God!

SCRIPTURE REFERENCES:

And take the helmet of salvation, and the sword of the Spirit, which is the word of God:
(Ephesians 6:17)

Thy word is a lamp unto my feet, and a light unto my path. **(Psalm 119:105)**

Bless the LORD, ye his angels, that excel in strength, that do his commandments, hearkening unto the voice of his word. **(Psalm 103:20)**

Then said he unto me, Fear not, Daniel: for from the first day that thou didst set thine heart to understand, and to chasten thyself before thy God, thy words were heard, and I am come for thy words.
(Daniel 10:12)

DAY #10: RELEASE A WAR CRY!

The Lord is fighting on your behalf! As you storm every demonic gate, open your mouth and declare your victory in the name of Jesus! Usher a war cry - a cry of victory into the atmosphere.

#ACryOfVictory

READ THIS PRAYER IN FAITH AND BELIEVE GOD TO MANIFEST YOUR BREAKTHROUGH:

Father God, in the name of Jesus, I overcome every limitation. I overcome every demonic gate in the name of Jesus. I thank You for empowering me to storm the gates of divine access and defeat every enemy assigned to stop me as I possess greater and greater realms of glory. I thank You that You have given me an unstoppable anointing and that I am able to possess and lay hold of every precious promise you have released over my life.

I release a war cry of victory as I take back everything that the enemy ever stole from me. I thank You that as I enter each realm and dimension that You would give me the wisdom to possess the treasures of the kingdom; greater wisdom, greater power, greater authority and a greater glory. I thank You for empowering me to break through the enemies lines and regain the spoils of war. I thank You that you have broken me through to a greater dimension in You!

Thank you for the victory in the mighty name of Jesus...I pray this powerful prayer in the name of Jesus! AMEN!

Your Breakthrough Is In Your Praise!

SCRIPTURE REFERENCES:

The Lord will go forth like a warrior,
He will stir up His zeal like a man of war;
He will shout out, yes, He will raise a war cry.
He will prevail [mightily] against His enemies.
(Isaiah 42:13)

For the LORD your God is he that goeth with you, to
fight for you against your enemies, to save you.
(Deuteronomy 20:4)

DAY #11: GIVE GOD THANKS FOR THE VICTORY!

This day is a day of thanksgiving as the spirit of the Lord gives you the victory. Your heart of thanksgiving keeps heaven open over you and moves the hand of God on your behalf in future battles.

#FeelingThankful

READ THIS PRAYER IN FAITH AND BELIEVE GOD TO MANIFEST YOUR BREAKTHROUGH:

Father God, in the name of Jesus I want to thank You for your mercy, Your power and Your grace. I thank you because I am grateful that You heard my cry once again and gave me the victory. I thank you that You have fought and again won the victory for me.

- *I thank You that You saved me, healed me and delivered me.*

- *I thank You for keeping heaven open over me.*

- *I thank You for moving on my behalf.*

- *I thank You for taking me higher in You.*

- *I thank You for delivering me from the enemy that was too strong for me.*

- *I thank You for subduing every enemy under my feet.*

- *I thank You for empowering me to break through every demonic barrier and gain divine access to the blessings of God.*

- *I thank You for anointing me to not just break in but allowing me to break through and come out with the victory.*

- *I thank You, that You will continue to gird me with strength for every spiritual battle.*

- *I thank You for it was You who fought for me and never left me to fight alone.*

Thank God For Your Breakthrough!

SCRIPTURE REFERENCES:

Be careful for nothing; but in everything by prayer and supplication with thanksgiving let your requests be made known unto God.
(Philippians 4:6)

I will praise thee: for thou hast heard me, and art become my salvation.
(Psalm 118:21)

In every thing give thanks: for this is the will of God in Christ Jesus concerning you.
(1 Thessalonians 5:18)

DAY #12: DAY OF ABSOLUTE BREAKTHROUGH AND ESTABLISHMENT

Anticipate total victory as God releases the answers to your prayers, and the spiritual attainment of greater dimensions in God as a result of your *12 Minutes To Breakthrough Prayer Strategy*.

#ATimeOfRest

READ THIS PRAYER IN FAITH AND BELIEVE GOD TO MANIFEST YOUR BREAKTHROUGH:

Father God, in the name of Jesus You have given me the victory, You have caused me to triumph over my enemies and You have blessed me to walk in a greater dimension in You.

You said that You would lead me beside still waters, You would restore my soul and that You would bless me with Your presence.

And now, O Lord I ask that You would restore me and during my times of refreshing in Your presence You will anoint me to fight another day. It is to You I give all glory, honor and praise as I rest in Your presence. I pray this prayer, in Jesus name. AMEN!

This Is Your Season Of Breakthrough!

SCRIPTURE REFERENCES:

*Now thanks be unto God, which always causeth us
to triumph in Christ, and maketh manifest the
savour of his knowledge by us in every place.*
(2 Corinthians 2:14)

*"...in thy presence is fullness of joy; at thy right
hand there are pleasures for evermore."*
(Psalm 16:11)

*For God alone my soul waits in silence and quietly
submits to Him, For my hope is from Him.*
(Psalm 62:5)

Rest in the Lord, and wait patiently for him.
(Psalm 37:7)

THE 12 MINUTES TO BREAKTHROUGH MINUTE-TO-MINUTE DAILY PRAYER ROUTINE

#1: YOUR FIRST MINUTE: As you come before God, strip yourself of pride, self and every sin that would seek to keep you bound. Purge your spiritual womb from the cares of this life, doubt, fear, and unbelief in preparation for the Spirit of God.

#2: YOUR SECOND MINUTE: The Word of God says that we are to enter His gates with thanksgiving and into His courts with praise, be thankful unto Him and bless His name. In order to create an atmosphere for the spirit of God, we must be prepared to offer Him praise and worship. During this time, you acknowledge that He is Lord and that He is able to solve your dilemma.

#3: YOUR THIRD MINUTE: As you elevate in the realm of the spirit, you will gain access into more profound realms and dimensions. Continue to give God praise and worship as you seek to attain greater realms of victory in Him.

#4: YOUR FOURTH MINUTE: As you build momentum in the realm of the spirit, employ the prophetic action of marching to demonstrate a military action which says that you are ready to engage the battle.

#5: YOUR FIFTH MINUTE: Continue your prophetic march and incorporate moving your fist in the air. This prophetic action demonstrates the Battleaxe Strategy which says that you have begun to aggressively confront your enemy. David was not only a king in Israel but he was also a skilled warrior. In ***Psalm 144:1***, David acknowledged God as The One who taught his hands to do war and his fingers to fight.

#6: YOUR SIXTH MINUTE: As you intensify your prophetic action, also intensify your heavenly language as you begin to gain grounds through the second heaven, or where satan's throne is set up. Your goal is the third dimension where the throne room of God is and where your breakthrough lies.

#7: YOUR SEVENTH MINUTE: During this minute of the Breakthrough Strategy is your most intense time. As you continue to elevate in the realm of the spirit you are seeking to break through demonic distractions, interceptions, hindrances and other demonic resistance. Your press is the hardest. Your push is the greatest. Your enemy seeks to stop you from breaking through to the third dimension, the throne room of God where your miracle lies. You must intensify, break through demonic barriers and gain access to your miracle.

#8: YOUR EIGHTH MINUTE: Your shout is synonymous to your war cry. You are fully engaged in battle. You are ascending in the realm of the spirit and the enemy is releasing his greatest resistance against you. As you lift up your voice with a shout, this confuses the enemy and sends a message to heaven that you are in desperate need of urgent help from your Savior, Deliverer and Sovereign King. Your shout engages Heaven in your battle. Your shout will bring supernatural intervention and miraculous victory.

#9: YOUR NINTH MINUTE: Once you have lifted your voice with a shout, captured Heaven's attention and dispelled every demonic interference, you can now present your case before God (a Heavenly Court).Begin to declare the Word of God as it relates to your situation. It is the declared word of God that gets heaven's attention and employs angels to work on your behalf. The angel that visits Daniel in *Daniel 3* told him that He had come because of his words. Your words can command angels to come to your rescue or move on your behalf. *Psalm 103:20* says to *bless ye His angels who move at the word of His command.*

#10: YOUR TENTH MINUTE: In humility as you travail in His presence, you make your requests known. Put Him in remembrance of His covenants and promises to you. Regardless of what you may have done, God is faithful and ready to forgive whatever wrong you may have done and move on your behalf.

#11: YOUR ELEVENTH MINUTE: Once you are confident that God has heard your prayer and has sent the answer, lift your voice and continue to give Him praise. Your attitude of thanksgiving will keep heaven open over you and touches the heart of God to move on your behalf when you are faced with your next battle.

#12: YOUR TWELFTH MINUTE: At your twelfth minute of prayer, you will sense breakthrough. Have faith that your victory is won, take a moment to "soak" and wait in His presence. *Psalm 37:7,* the Word of God says *to rest in the Lord and wait patiently for Him.* Appreciate Him for what He has done and celebrate Him for who He is. Prepare to leave the battleground victorious as you gain your miracle and God gets the glory. Please note that your soak period may take you beyond the 12-minute time frame. You are free to lay prostrate before the Lord.

THE 12 MINUTES TO BREAKTHROUGH VICTORY

This powerful, impacting *12 Minute to Breakthrough Prayer and Spiritual Warfare Strategy* is guaranteed to bring some level of supernatural breakthrough and victory once implemented strategically. The Word of God says that God is in tuned to the cry of the righteous; He hears and He sends the answers.

This Prayer Strategy will empower you to break through the demonic gates of your enemy, bombard the gates of heaven and come forth victorious in times of spiritual combat. Your victory is sure once you pray consistently at *12 noon and 12 midnight for 12 minutes over a period of 12 days.*

YOU MADE IT!

✳✳✳✳✳✳✳✳✳✳✳✳✳✳✳✳✳✳✳

CONSISTENT, PERSISTENT PRAYER NOT ONLY CHANGES THINGS BUT CAUSES THINGS TO CHANGE IN YOUR FAVOR!

— *Apostle Edison Nottage*

THE 12 MINUTES TO PROPHETIC BREAKTHROUGH PRAYER
"Breaking Through To Your Next Level In God!"

Pray this prayer with authority and watch God work miraculously and supernaturally on your behalf:

Father, God in the name of Jesus I stand before you in the power of your Word for Hebrews 4:16 says that I can come boldly before the throne of grace to find mercy in the time of need. I thank you, Lord, for your goodness, your mercy and grace. I bless you as my Deliverer, my Redeemer and my Savior. I praise you as Lord and Sovereign Ruler.

Now, Father cleanse me from all unrighteousness; purify my heart, my thoughts and my mind; wash me now in the blood of Jesus from the crown of my head to the soles of my feet. If it had not been for You who was on my side, I would have been consumed.

But Thou has been my help, O Lord! Anoint me again, strengthen me again with power from on high; remove every burden, destroy every yoke of the enemy in the name of Jesus.

I come against every plan of the enemy for my life right now, in the name of Jesus.

I cancel every diabolical strategy and tactic of the enemy that would seek to keep me in bondage.

12 MINUTES TO BREAKTHROUGH

I come against ever demonic oppression that is seeking to hinder my progress right now, in the name of Jesus.

I destroy every demonic resistance that has been sent to frustrate my progress.

I reverse every curse of the enemy that has been sent to resist me.

I come against every demonic spirit of sabotage that would seek to destroy my destiny, and I release the fire of God against my enemies.

Let every demonic plan backfire by fire, in the name of Jesus. Drive my enemies away, O Lord; stand up for my help, O mighty God. '

You are Jehovah Jireh, the God who goes before me in the way and makes every provision for my victory.

You are Jehovah Gibhor, Mighty Warrior and God of War; warfare now against my enemies.

You are Jehovah Sabbaoth, the Lord of hosts and the God of armies; command now your angels to fight on my behalf.

I dispatch war angels with swords of fire to fight against every demonic prince that is seeking to stop me.

I dispatch Michael, the warring archangel, to fight on my behalf right now, in the name of Jesus.

I release this prayer as a battering ram in the realm of the spirit and break through to my next level in God.

I thank you, Lord, that You are taking me through levels, realms and dimensions in You.

By Your mighty hand I can run through a troop and leap over walls.

By Your mighty hand I am blessed going out and blessed coming in.

By Your mighty hand I have been made the head and not the tail.

By Your mighty hand I have broken through the enemy's lines and have won the battle this day.

Send now prosperity, in the name of Jesus. Send now Your power, O mighty God.

Your Word says it is Your good pleasure to give me the kingdom; open unto me now Your good treasure, O Lord; according to Your loving kindness, bless me, indeed!

I thank You for hearing my prayer. I give You all the praise, glory and honor for a mighty victory this day, in the name of Jesus I pray! AMEN!

INDEX

PROPHET DR. MATTIE NOTTAGE BA, MA, DD
MINISTRY PROFILE

Widely endorsed as a prophet to the nations, God has used Dr. Mattie Nottage to captivate audiences around the world through her insightful, life-changing messages. Dr. Nottage is married to Apostle Edison Nottage. She co-pastors, along with her husband, Believers Faith Outreach Ministries, International in Nassau, Bahamas.

Mantled with an uncanny spirit of discernment and an undeniable prophetic anointing, Dr. Nottage is a well-respected international preacher, prolific teacher, kingdom ambassador, motivational speaker, life coach, playwright, author, gospel recording artist and revivalist. She is the President and Founder of *Mattie Nottage Ministries, International, The Global Dominion Network Empowering Group of Companies, The Youth In Action Group and The Faith Village For Girls Transformation Program. She is also The Chancellor of The Mattie Nottage School of Ministry. She is the Founder of the prestigious Mattie Nottage Outstanding Kingdom Woman's Award.*

Dr. Nottage has ministered the gospel, in places such as: Ireland, Brazil, Africa, The Netherlands, throughout the United States of America and The Caribbean. Gifted with an authentic anointing, God uses her to "set the captive free" and to fan the flames of revival throughout the nations. Dr. Mattie Nottage has an endearing passion to train and equip individuals to advance the Kingdom of God and walk in total victory.

She is the author of her bestselling books, ***"Breaking The Chains, From Worship to Warfare", "I Refuse To Die" and "Secrets Every Mother Should Tell Her Daughter About Life" Book & Journal.***

Dr. Nottage is also a regular columnist in The Tribune, the national newspaper of the Bahamas. She has also written numerous publications, stage plays and songs, including the #1 smash hit CD Singles, *"I Refuse To Die In This Place!"*, *"The Verdict Is In...Not Guilty!"* and *"I Still Want You!"*

She has regularly appeared as a guest on various television networks including The Trinity Broadcasting Network (TBN), The Word Network, The Atlanta Live TV and The Babbie Mason Talk Show "Babbie's House." Additionally, Dr. Mattie Nottage has been featured in several publications such as the Preaching Woman Magazine and the "Gospel Today" Magazine as one of America's most influential pastors. She, along with her husband, Apostle Edison are the hosts of their very own television broadcast, "Transforming Lives".

Dr. Nottage is the former Chairman of the National Youth Advisory Council to the government of the Bahamas and was also recognized and awarded a *"Proclamation of State" by the Mayor and Commissioner of Miami-Dade County, Florida* for her exemplary community initiatives which brought transformation and empowerment to the lives of youth and families globally.

Further, Dr. Nottage has earned her Bachelor of Arts degree in Christian Counseling, a Masters of Arts degree in Christian Education, and a Doctor of Divinity degree from the renown St. Thomas University, in Jacksonville, Florida and is also a graduate of Kingdom University. Additionally, she has earned her Certified Life Coaching Degree from the F. W. I. Life Coach Training Institute. Dr. Mattie Nottage is known as a Trailblazer and a *Doctor of Deliverance* who is committed and dedicated to *Breaking Chains and Transforming Lives!*

POWERFUL PROPHETIC PRAYERS

- FROM WORSHIP TO WARFARE · SPIRITUAL WARFARE PRAYER PART 1

- FROM WORSHIP TO WARFARE · SPIRITUAL WARFARE PRAYER PART 2

- PROPHETIC BREAKTHROUGH PRAYER PART 1

- PROPHETIC BREAKTHROUGH PRAYER PART 2

- PROPHETIC BREAKTHROUGH PRAYER OF DECLARATION

- PRAYER FOR PROGRESS & ACTIVATION FOR FAMILIES AND CHILDREN

- PRAYER FOR FINANCIAL BREAKTHROUGH

- PRAYER OF HEALING FOR THE WOUNDED SOUL

- MORNING PRAYER OF BLESSING

- WARFARE AGAINST THE SEED OF THE SERPENT

ORDER YOUR COPY TODAY!

Also Available

Music CD

Music CD Single "I Refuse To Die"
This prophetic song of hope and healing is an anthem to encourage you to live a life of victory overcoming every challenge or adversity of the enemy. Get your copy today and make a prophetic declaration through song that you "Refuse To Die!"

Prayer CD

Prayer of Deliverance for the Wounded Soul

Breaking the Spirit of Limitation

To request Dr. Mattie Nottage for a speaking engagement, upcoming event, life coaching seminar, mentorship session or to place an order for products, please contact:

Mattie Nottage Ministries, International (Bahamas Address)

P.O. Box SB-52524
Nassau, N. P. Bahamas
Tel/Fax: (242) 698-1383 or
(954) 237-8196

OR

Mattie Nottage Ministries, International (U.S. Address)

6511 Nova Dr., Suite #193
Davie, Florida 33317

Tel/Fax: **(888) 825-7568**

OR
www.mattienottage.org

Follow us on:
Facebook @ DrMattie Nottage
and Twitter @ DrMattieNottage

Made in the USA
Coppell, TX
20 April 2021